Christopher Esget is the consummate parish pastor. He warns us against our disordered world and sets before us God's reordering of all things in Christ. We face what we think of as new challenges to the faith of the Church and the piety of her children. Esget shows that the ancient revelation of God in Christ, delivered once and for all through the Word of the prophets and apostles, responds to all these challenges with grace, encouragement, and comfort for the troubled soul. This is soul care at its best!

Scott R. Murray, PhD, senior pastor, Memorial Lutheran Church; vice president, LCMS West Southwest Region

In 1983, Nobel Prize recipient Aleksandr Solzhenitsyn delivered the most memorable speech of his distinguished career. He said the decline of great civilizations commence when "men have forgotten God." In Christopher Esget's magnificent new book, he demonstrates that the vigorous cultural and societal war being prosecuted against natural law norms has consequences propelling the destruction of marriages, families, and children. Repudiation and rebellion are the sad, recurring motifs. Yet the glory of Esget's powerful analysis is that Christian hope and the seeds of authentic regeneration are possible even in a spiritual desert where transgressive ideas seem omnipresent. This is a must-read book, worthy of Solzhenitsyn's matchless rigor, intellectual goodness, and moral duty to be intelligent.

Timothy S. Goeglein, vice president, External and Government Relations, Focus on the Family

In recent years, there have been many attempts to explain how our discourse became dominated by destructive ideas such as Marxism, transgenderism, emotivism, and plain old narcissism. But nearly all those explanations have failed to discuss the true and singular antidote to our ideological ailments—the Gospel of Jesus Christ. With stunning clarity, Esget has written a highly accessible book that brings together theology, politics, and culture to deliver the message that a light shines in the darkness and no "ism" can overcome it.

Mollie Ziegler Hemingway, editor in chief, *The Federalist*

(DIS)ORDERED

Lies about Human Nature and the Truth That Sets Us Free

CHRISTOPHER S. ESGET

CONCORDIA PUBLISHING HOUSE • SAINT LOUIS

Published by Concordia Publishing House
3558 S. Jefferson Avenue, St. Louis, MO 63118-3968
1-800-325-3040 • cph.org

Manufactured in the United States of America

1 2 3 4 5 6 7 8 9 10   32 31 30 29 28 27 26 25 24 23

CONTENTS

INTRODUCTION

I first began serving as a pastor in 1998 at Bethel Lutheran Church in DuQuoin, Illinois. There I was blessed with a number of wonderful colleagues, pastors who served as elder brothers, friends, and mentors. Three in particular invited me to play golf with them every Monday. It was a happy time in my life, but also one where my faith was shaken. Two of these pastors were on their own theological pilgrimages away from our church's teaching, and I was tempted to follow them. The last conversation I had with one of them shortly before he left the area challenged the bedrock of my own understanding of what the Bible teaches. Part of my friend's rejection of our church's teaching was his rejection of original sin. I agreed with him on so much; could I be wrong about this?

It later became the subject of a thesis for my second master's degree, under Rev. Dr. David P. Scaer at Concordia Theological Seminary, Fort Wayne, Indiana. Through the next four years, I read everything I could about original sin and came to the conclusion that without it, the Bible makes no sense, and there is no need for a Redeemer, no need for the atonement.

Around the same time, I began to notice that my parishioners didn't seem to believe in the resurrection of the body. Funeral after funeral, I encountered Christians with a truncated eschatology: a person dies and goes to heaven. End of story.

Except that's not the end of the story. The creeds end with the resurrection of the body, and Revelation ends with a new creation. Preaching and teaching about the resurrection became an obsession for me. I began to see both of these doctrines—original sin and the resurrection of the body—as two sides of the same doctrinal coin: sin brought death into the world, the resurrection of Jesus is the firstfruits of our own coming resurrection, when the curse of death will be abolished.

In 2001, my wife, Kassie, and I moved to the suburbs of Washington, DC, where I was called to be the pastor of Immanuel Evangelical Lutheran Church in Alexandria, Virginia. I'd been pro-life since the time my mother took me as a young boy with her to volunteer at a secondhand shop where the proceeds went to a local women's support center. The notion that some mothers chose to abort their children shocked me, as it does every child who first learns the truth. One of my earliest "dates" with Kassie was at a pro-life demonstration in Norman, Oklahoma. Now just outside the nation's capital, I started becoming connected with the national pro-life movement.

During this time, my wife and I struggled with barrenness and the devastation of a miscarriage. Every January, my wife and I marched to the Supreme Court for the rights of babies to live, while longing for a baby of our own to love. On the road that eventually led us to adoption, I read and thought a great deal about the meaning of marriage and sex.

Other changes were happening while I was thinking about these issues of original sin, the resurrection, and what it means to be married. The US government embraced homosexual "marriage." Legal battles ensued over new mandates for Christian business owners and even nuns to pay for contraception. The transgender movement aggressively changed the fields of law, medicine, and education while also demanding radical changes to the English language. Race relations that had been improving for decades in America rapidly collapsed.

What do all these issues have to do with one another? They are all intrinsically related to what it means to be human. Marriage, sex (both kinds: being male or female, and the bodily intimacy that was once reserved exclusively for marriage), childbearing, and the families (ethnic groups) of the earth united by a common humanity—all are under assault. We are witnessing a seismic shift in human history, an assault on the foundations of human nature and society. This book began as my attempt to show how the loss of a conception of original sin is connected to all these cultural challenges. Over the course of writing it, I came to see something more: a diabolical plot to reconfigure the world around a new religion disconnected from creation. If "diabolical plot" sounds overly dramatic, I invite you to read Genesis 3; Matthew 4:1–11; and Revelation 12. Some things are not new. The diabolical plot has been unfolding since the dragon, Satan, offered our first parents the opportunity to become like God, knowing good and evil. Pharaoh and Herod both killed babies in an attempt to destroy God's promise. The sexual lives of Abraham, Jacob, David, and Solomon were all . . . questionable. But with transgenderism, we've entered into something new: the radical reconfiguration of the idea of humanity.

A corresponding threat to humanity is the new form of Marxism that has captured American academia. The ideology that in the twentieth century caused the murder of tens of millions of people in the Soviet Union alone has been repackaged for the training seminars of the United States government and most major corporations.

Public school children are being inculcated in it, teaching them to see the world as divided up into groups of oppressors and oppressed.

These various ideologies (LGBTQ and cultural Marxism) have joined forces. In their goal of reshaping society, they aim for the abolition of Christianity. The threat is extraordinary, and this book details various facets of it. But with great threat comes great opportunity. The Church, becoming once again persecuted, will learn anew that discipleship is no mere checking of boxes: Baptism, periodic church attendance, and keeping up an appearance of morality in public. The ancient Jews were criticized for being circumcised in body but not in heart. For too many of us, Christianity has been an organization and a set of activities, but not a radical commitment to following Jesus and living from His Word and Sacraments. These challenges offer us an opportunity to learn again what it means to be married, what it means to hope in the resurrection, what it means to live in community—in short, what it means to be human.

This book is divided into two parts. In the first part, I explore how the Western mind became psychologized, overdeveloping a concept of the human self rooted in thinking instead of embodiment. Then I set forth what God's Word says about man's purpose and how our disconnection from the created order is causing our society to degenerate. Along the way, I set out the ramifications of the fall and how the fear of death holds us in bondage. Chapters 4 through 7 outline the contemporary challenges to a biblical worldview, particularly extreme narcissism, the eroticizing of everything, pornography, abortion, homosexuality, transgenderism, and racism.

In the second part, on how we can be healed from these maladies, I begin with Christ and His work of bringing human nature to its goal. Then I discuss a better way to think about sex, the danger of following our passions, and a warning about demons. The book concludes with the New Testament vision for a renewed humanity in the resurrection and new creation.

I am grateful to Pete Jurchen and Laura Lane at Concordia Publishing House for all their help, guidance, and patience in getting this book from idea to publication. Thanksgiving is due to my amazing seminary professors whose words and writings are still teaching me, especially Arthur Just, David Scaer, William Weinrich, and Dean Wenthe. I must thank my Bishop, Jamison Hardy, for his unwavering support of me, as well as the leaders of The Lutheran Church—Missouri Synod for their prayers and friendship: Matthew Harrison, Peter Lange, John Wohlrabe, Scott Murray, Nabil Nour, and Ben Ball. My amazing congregation has supported and cared for me for more than twenty-one years and provided me time off to work on this book. I owe a particular debt of gratitude to Leo Mackay, Andy Scheck, and Aaron Lewis, along with the staff at Immanuel, whose patience has been tested while I completed this book: Sherry Graveson, Julia Habrecht, Stephanie Mekonen, and Noah Rogness.

Finally, I am forever grateful to my family: my mother, Eileen, and my late father, Leo, for teaching me to be a Christian and loving me unconditionally; my mother-in-law, Karen Adams; my son, James, who daily teaches me grace; and most especially my dear wife, Kassie, who ceaselessly shows me love, patience, and encouragement.

PART I

THE CONTAGION
INFECTING HUMANITY

CHAPTER 1

THE AUTHENTIC SELF

Introduction

Underlying the rapid changes in today's society—particularly the acceptance of homosexual "marriage" and the celebration of transgenderism—is a more fundamental question: What does it mean to be human? Descartes's famous dictum *cogito ergo sum* ("I think, therefore I am") began a philosophical cascade of rooting man's identity within his own mind: my cogitation defines me. Our society is in the process of replacing truth with feelings, and unmooring sex from marriage. This is a central cause of the profound instability we all feel in Western culture. It is unlike anything we have experienced in living memory. Today, our society seems to be focusing more on feelings than thoughts. This is resulting in instability in established institutions like marriage and human sexuality.

People are searching for authenticity, but that search is only leading them away from the Author. We are disconnected and discontent, and someone must bear the blame. Into this void, a doctrine of demons is becoming the state religion. The catechists of this religion have doctrines of sin that obscenely reverse the Ten Commandments. At the core of this new religion is the rejection of a God who creates and a mankind who receives life from the One who made them. This chapter will examine how the doctrines of this new religion have developed, and will also set forth man's true nature, purpose, and destiny.

Psychological Man

What is a person? Previous periods in history saw man either characterized as primarily a religious creature or a creature defined by the marketplace (*homo economicus*). Recent history has seen a change from a materialist definition of the person—You are what you eat—to people defining themselves by psychological experience: You are what you feel.

The beginnings of this may be found in the Jesuit philosopher René Descartes (1596–1650). Descartes believed that man's mind is entirely distinct from his body. If thinking proves existence, then ideas are above and outside of concrete realities. This sets the stage for the radical autonomy of self-creation: if I exist because I think, my thinking generates my existence and defines it. By contrast, running counter to this popular belief, the sixteenth-century reformers of the church confessed that thinking, feeling, and sensing were all part of a unified human person. The creator united body and soul, physical existence and the life of the mind: "I believe that God has made me and all creatures; that He has given me my body and soul, eyes, ears, and all my members, my reason and all my senses, and still takes care of them."[1]

For today's psychological man, feeling has replaced thinking. Feelings define meanings. Feelings give identity and purpose. To be authentic, to reach his *telos* (life's goal—more on that later), he believes he must embrace his feelings and take them to their conclusion. Feelings belong uniquely to the self. They are his truth, and thus no one can tell psychological man he is wrong. Moral decisions are entirely based on preference.

In this view, there can be no external, objective purpose to the world. The common cultural assumptions once shared in the

---

1   Small Catechism, First Article of the Apostles' Creed.

United States (and more broadly, with Canada, Europe, and Australia) are gone, replaced with . . . nothing. This renders relationships with others meaningless—except in how they help one fulfill one's own meaning, especially as sex partners. Here the legacy of psychologist Sigmund Freud (1856–1939) looms large, telling us we are, at our core, sexual beings. If psychological man is defined by what he feels, psychosexual man is defined by what he desires sexually. There can be no debate since there is no transcendent meaning, no shared code or text or story. In the history of the world, this is unique. We are in uncharted territory.

The cultural instability we are experiencing is not unlike that period of time after a riot breaks out but before the police arrive. Except, in this case, the police are not coming.

The Quest for Authenticity

God's Word teaches us how to think about ourselves: "Know that the LORD, He is God! It is He who made us, and we are His" (Psalm 100:3). This can also be translated "It is He who made us, and not we ourselves."[2] The contemporary quest for "authenticity" turns this on its head: "It is I who make me, and no one else."

The notion of personal authenticity derives from the philosophical school of existentialism, a term originating from the work of Danish Lutheran Søren Kierkegaard (1813–1855). Twentieth-century existentialists include Albert Camus (1913–1960), Martin Heidegger (1889–1976), and John-Paul Sartre (1905–80). Existentialism looks for meaning in personal experience rather than reason, although absurdity plays a strong role: the world is pointless and without meaning. In the existentialist world, being human is to make self-conscious choices. You are what you choose. To be true to yourself, do what you desire.

2   See the translation note on Psalm 100:3 in the English Standard Version Bible.

15

Our culture is deeply steeped in this way of thinking. One need never have heard of the terms or the philosophers; existentialism is encoded in the slogans peppering our eyes and ears, such as "My body, my choice," "Have it your way," and "The only truth is what you decide for yourself." Live your own truth, but don't you dare impose it on another.

The authentic life, in such a worldview, is the one that comes from within yourself. Here psychotherapy comes into play. Through talk therapy, the therapist helps the individual find his or her truth and then strengthen his or her courage to act on what is discovered. Thus the stage is set for a man to proclaim himself a woman—or a penguin, or a puppy. Once authenticity becomes disconnected from biological reality, it is not so easily reconnected. We are living in a world that is in rebellion against the Creator. This rebellion is not on the margins, bending certain rules. Rather, the very core of a givenness to creation is rejected, as the world lashes out at God, "It is not You who made me, but I myself." My authenticity becomes how I publicly express myself, especially sexually. If I keep my sexual desires private, I commit the societal sin of inauthenticity. Being "true to yourself" means making private desires public; the moment of authenticity is lauded as "coming out." Whereas God's Word sees pride as the chief vice, the teaching of the world makes pride the chief virtue. The world's obligation is no longer to correct and restrain impulses, but to celebrate them. Failure to thus celebrate is bigotry. Thus the new individualistic society exists to affirm individuals' psychological desires (and pay for their maintenance, as needed, through hormone treatments and surgery). The fundamental problem, in the view of the sexual revolutionaries, lies in preexisting societal conventions. Any imposition upon the individual through expectations of following the preexisting sexual code or conforming to those standards is a denial of freedom for the individual to flourish. Those age-old social expectations are tantamount to slavery. Only the inauthentic allow themselves to be guided by preexisting societal norms.

Self-creation requires each person's life to be unique, distinct from all others, and authentic. The body becomes the canvas—with social media the gallery—for each person's artistic expression. The radical reconfiguring of the body is seen in transgenderism, yet it happens in a myriad of small ways too. Tattoos, piercings, and cosmetic surgery to change the size and shape of noses, breasts, and lips—all reflect the modern desire to customize and refashion the body, discontent with its created givenness.

The experience of discontent, the loss of rootedness and identity, reflects the underlying terrifying thought that everything is meaningless. "All is vanity," says Solomon in Ecclesiastes 1:2, reflecting the experience of life as futile and frustrating. Without a Creator, there is no order in creation. Without an understanding of humanity's fall into sin, man must find someone or something to blame for this experience.

Original Sins

To affix blame, the cultural and sexual revolutionaries have created a parody of the Christian religion, with new devils and new crimes to function as the original sin. Whereas Christianity sees original sin as damaging every human being (see chapters 2 and 3), sociopolitical uses of original sin place it in particular races, societal structures, and institutions. In the Marxist scheme, those who possess the means of production—the capitalists—are oppressing the people. Neo-Marxist thought now identifies slavery as the original sin of the United States, and the people groups who did not experience slavery as the original sinners. In other words, original sin is not a power or tendency within all people but a condition dividing the world into oppressors and oppressed, sinners and those sinned against. In this scheme, there is no room for repentance, atonement, and reconciliation (ideas all deeply rooted in the Sacred Scriptures). The societal structures that have perpetuated the original sin must be destroyed. Neo-Marxism married with the sexual revolution seeks to overthrow the traditional family. There can be no laissez-faire, live-and-let-live attitude that allows traditional Christian moral views to stand alongside the sexual revolution. The very existence of the commandment "You shall not commit adultery" is not simply outmoded but is also viewed as an existential threat to human freedom. Christianity is "thought-crime."

If you wonder why the world seems to be going crazy, it's because the worldview I've just described—man is by nature good, but the traditional societal structure is evil—now fills the minds of many. Christians, who see themselves and all people as sinful, will not easily have a rational discussion with those who think so differently. There is no agreement on first principles—on what is sin, what is righteousness, and what kind of judgment (see John 16:8–11) is necessary or even possible.

At the risk of oversimplifying, we can divide our society into three epistemologies:[3] those who combine natural knowledge of the world (via observation and deductions derived from the scientific method of inquiry) with a trust in the revealed knowledge from God (through the prophets and sacred writings); those who rely only on natural knowledge; and those who believe that the only truth that can be known is through feelings. Classical Chris-

---

3   Epistemology is the theory of how something can be known.

tianity belongs to the first group; the second group we can broadly call rationalists; the third group I term emotivists.[4] If you've ever heard someone speak about "your truth" or "my truth," you know you're dealing with an emotivist. That is the epistemology dominating today's cultural landscape. It has made deep inroads into Christianity as well, particularly where worship forms are utilized to elevate emotional experiences over God's Word. Those experiences then become the cause of faith and a ground of truth.

Some church leaders today also subject the Word of God to personal experiences and feelings. A common Bible study question, "What does this verse mean to you?" is in this category. The goal of the question is not to determine the objective meaning of what God has said. Instead, the subjective encounter of the reader or listener becomes the arbiter of truth. Another form of this emotivism is called *listening prayer*. Here the person may begin with a small passage of Scripture or some other devotional thought, and then spend time silently listening for what God is saying now to the individual. The Scriptures are demoted from their authority as inviolable Word of God and relegated to a catalyst for individuals to create their own truths, which stem from their inner thoughts. When you hear a person say, "The Lord said to me thus and so," and it isn't a simple affirmation of what the Bible says, you know you are dealing with a person who does not in practice affirm the Scriptures as sufficient for faith and life. Private experience trumps public revelation.

How then can you, a Christian, encounter the Scriptures as fully authoritative and inviolable, yet as a living Word that speaks to you today? It starts with the doctrine of Creation.

---

4   Alasdair MacIntyre (1929–) coined the term *emotivism* for the modern school of ethics that determines right and wrong by sentiment. See *After Virtue*, 3rd ed. (Notre Dame, IN: University of Notre Dame Press, 2007).

Creation

Christians derive their sense of meaning from the One who made us. He fills the world with meaning. Since "all things were made through Him" (John 1:3), our lives possess divine meaning and purpose. Man is the object of God's love. Lutheran theologian Johann Gerhard put it this way: "He saw that His goodness could be shared, and thus the streams of His goodness [flow] to His creatures, while the spring remains inexhaustible forever."[5] All created things, including man—the crown of God's creation—were made good. It is a derived goodness: man receives his goodness from his Maker.

Again and again, Moses says of God beholding His creation: "And God saw that it was good" (Genesis 1:10, 12, 18, 21, 25). Finally, at the creation of our first parents, "God saw everything that He had made, and behold, *it was* ***very good***" (v. 31, emphasis added)—good from God's lavish goodness.

This view cannot be overemphasized today because we are inundated with images of interchangeable or ephemeral bodies that are inferior to their disembodied human spirits that live on after the bodies' demise. Think of popular galactic-war-type movie franchises, where bodies disintegrate but spirits live on through a mystical force. Other popular science-fiction programs posit a consciousness that is uploaded to a computer to live on after death.

Do not discount these stories as harmless. Fiction affects faith. Listen to how people speak of the body after death, and you'll see similar thoughts at work. "I know I shouldn't be sad; it's just a shell," one widow sobbed as we stood before her husband's coffin in the funeral home. So deeply had she imbibed the cultural message of

---

5   Johann Gerhard, "On Creation and Angels" in vol. 8–11 of *Theological Commonplaces*, trans. Richard J. Dinda, ed. Benjamin T. G. Mayes and Joshua J. Hayes (St. Louis: Concordia Publishing House, 2013), 42 (§ 84).

the body being a "shell" for the true person, that her sadness confused her. If the body is ultimately meaningless, a mere container, then why sorrow at its death?

The reason is that death is a terrible sundering of what God made. He did not make us as spirits temporarily inhabiting bodies in a material world. The body and soul of the first man were designed as integral parts of one person. "The LORD God formed the man of dust from the ground and breathed into his nostrils the breath of life, and the man became a living creature" (Genesis 2:7). The material of the earth joined with God's breath of life constitutes one living creature. The Hebrew term *nephesh,* translated here by the ESV as "creature," is often rendered as "soul." This is instructive since many think of the soul as an immaterial aspect of the person, distinct and separate from the body. The term can be used that way, but this foundational part of God's Word teaches us that a person is not fully human apart from his body. Nor is he living apart from the living breath that comes from God. Man is a living creature—a living *soul*—by virtue of the Word and breath of God that animates his body.

This means that the material nature of man—his body—is good. Before death enters the world, God declares that the things He creates are good. Again and again, He sees what He makes— waters, plants, birds, fish, animals—and pronounces them good. The culmination of His creation is man and woman. This He declares not simply good, but "very good" (Genesis 1:31).

Yet man is unique among all the created things on earth. Nothing else in all creation receives the breath of God directly from Him. All other things God makes by His Word alone. For example, He says, "Let there be light," and there is light (Genesis 1:3). The first man is singularly fashioned by God from the matter of earth.

The first woman is made from the man's body, his opened side used as the originating material. Among all things made, our first parents are distinct from everything else. This special distinction God calls being made in His image and likeness.

Man's Original, Dynamic Purpose

What then was man's purpose? God expressed His goodness both in the creation of man and in the order and beauty of the garden into which our first parents were placed. Adam was not created for a static life but to maintain and expand upon the work God had done: "The Lord God took the man and put him in the garden of Eden to work it and keep it" (Genesis 2:15). Man had work to do. This is his first task.

After the creation of the woman and the institution of holy marriage, there is also the ongoing work of procreation: "Be fruitful and multiply and fill the earth and subdue it" (Genesis 1:28). This gift of marriage and children was not a burden but a blessing. In fact, the power of procreation is given specifically in a blessing: "And God blessed them. And God said to them, 'Be fruitful and multiply and fill the earth and subdue it'" (v. 28). The blessing of sex—not the activity, but the identity, that is, of being specifically male or female—is in the gift of relationship. In God's design, one is not sexual in isolation. "It is not good that the man should be alone" (Genesis 2:18). Even for those with strictly heterosexual attractions, God's design was not for a generic attraction to the opposite sex. God's gift of sex within marriage is unique in that God designed it to be a self-giving and procreative act between spouses.

The nature of the attraction (i.e., being attracted to the same sex instead of the opposite sex), then, is not the biggest problem in human sexuality. Having the mind not in conformity with the body (i.e., lacking a sense of contentment and psychological wellness in identifying with one's biological sex) is also not the biggest problem in human sexuality. These are symptoms of the larger problem faced by every human person: we want sex to gratify our personal desires instead of to give ourselves to another. Virtually everyone, regardless of inclinations or fetishes, is selfish when it comes to sex. That's the problem.

God made us for relational sexuality. Within a sexual relationship, the man is to be the husband of one wife and to fulfill the role of provider, guardian, and father for a specific family. Within a sexual relationship, the woman is to be the wife of one man and to fulfill the role of nurturing spouse and mother for a specific family. Thus, the marriage vows call for living together. In society today, the phrase "living together" is shorthand for having sexual relations together and sharing a residence without being married. From the divine perspective, however, the only true living together is when the lives of husband and wife are so united that they are one flesh and find their purpose in living for the benefit of the family. That is profoundly different from sharing a bed and some of the bills. What I am saying is this: sex is inherently relational. For an individual to self-identify according to sexual attraction is the epitome of self-worship (or, to use the language of the next chapter, of being "curved in on the self"). Only in the marital relationship of sexual self-giving can God-given dominion (Genesis 1:28) occur.

This work of dominion is easily misunderstood; *dominion* in contemporary English often has the nuance of unkindness, the victor vanquishing (*dominating*) an enemy. It is better to think of this, however, as man continuing the work of God on the earth. God is the Lord—in Latin, *dominus*—and dominion is bringing His lordship to bear on the wild places of the earth.

Since God's nature is love (1 John 4:8), His dominion is the infusion of love into every aspect of creation. Consider: Why did God make man in the first place? One early Christian teacher, Irenaeus of Lyons (martyred ca. AD 202), beautifully answers this question: it was to have someone on whom to give His benefits.[6] In other words, God wanted someone to love, someone to receive His gifts, someone to share His joy in all His works.

If you have children, you probably know the joy of giving, of making them glad. At first, we may desire children for selfish purposes: to carry on our legacy, to fulfill our goals, to reflect our own image. The arrival of children reveals a great challenge to our selfishness: children need our benefits: clothing and shoes, house and home, food and drink, toys and medicine, and most important, time. Loving parents rejoice to provide, often foregoing purchases for themselves in order to give what they have to their children. Children teach parents self-giving. In this, the parents are learning something of God's nature.

God transferred this desire for self-giving from His heart to within our first parents, guiding them by His words to "have dominion." Within this world, man's work was to spread the dominion of God to every place. Because of the fall into sin, however, the idea of work is often compared to pain, burden, drudgery, and suffering. Work is considered a necessity, not a joy, and many fantasize about a life without work, like the man who tore down his barns to build bigger ones: "I will tear down my barns and build larger ones, and there I will store all my grain and my goods. And I will say to my soul, 'Soul, you have ample goods laid up for many years; relax, eat, drink, be merry'" (Luke 12:18–19).

In the beginning, it was not so. Work was meant to be deeply

---

6   See Irenaeus, *Against Heresies* 4.14.1.

satisfying, a joy. My friend Nabil is very skilled at making things from wood. He has a well-equipped woodshop in his basement, and when he is done with his obligations for the day, he spends time making everything from crosses to boats to toys for his grandchildren. It looks like work to me, but to him it is play. That is what the tasks God gave man to do are like: play, efforts that are deeply satisfying, such that we are glad when they are complete, not because the obligation has been checked off a to-do list, but because the outcome is pleasing. God made man for this kind of work: His work, in which we are privileged to participate. Participation—or to use a more scriptural term, *communion*—is why God made man. He made man to participate in His divine life.

Your Purpose: Growing to Perfection

Irenaeus spoke of Adam and Eve as children. They were created to grow and come to perfection.[7] The paradise God made for them was better than what we now experience, conducive to their growth. Whether this is true is difficult to say, but Irenaeus was not alone in seeing that man was created for more than a static existence. God intended man to grow and mature. Aquinas saw man (and all creation) as having a goal toward which we would grow: "So, too, every creature aims to achieve its own perfection, which is the likeness of God's perfection and goodness. Therefore divine goodness is the goal of all things."[8]

In a future chapter, we will see a strange thing said about the Christ, that He was "made perfect." If that sounds wrong, it's because many define perfection as moral goodness or perhaps purity. That doesn't seem to fit the Christian view of Christ, for at no time

7   See Irenaeus, *The Demonstration of the Apostolic Preaching*, ed. W. J. Sparrow Simpson and W. K. Lowther Clarke, trans. J. Armitage Robinson, in Translations of Christian Literature, Series 4, Oriental Texts (London; New York: Society for Promoting Christian Knowledge; The Macmillan Co., 1920), 81.
8   Thomas Aquinas, *Summa Theologica*, Part 1, Question 44, Article 4.

was the Second Person of the Trinity morally flawed or impure. However, there is another way to think about perfection: reaching maturity (or reaching a goal).

Think of the perfect piece of fruit, or the perfect tree. No doubt you formed an image in your mind of that thing fully formed: a ripened strawberry, not one just emerging. With an object that we make, its perfection is revealed in performing its proper task, like an airplane that takes off and lands without crashing or a baseball bat that hits the ball without splintering.

We might make something for a very specific task, like a rocket transport system to deliver a rover to explore the planet Mars and send back its findings. God made man for a specific purpose: to reflect His image and likeness, to be an embodiment of God's goodness, and ultimately to enjoy communion with Him. True authenticity is embracing our own givenness, including the time and location where God has placed us and the gifts and limitations He has bestowed on or withheld from us. We don't need to create (or re-create) ourselves to find our authenticity. It is found in the One who is our Author.

Post-Modern Man: Disconnected from Creation

Throughout much of history, humans—whether Christian or not—saw a sense of order in the world. Creation had a Creator, which meant the world had meaning. Men sought to discover the meaning of the world in nature and then act accordingly. This is sometimes called the *mimetic* view of the world.[9] Since God is the Maker, and man is the one who has been made, man thus derives the meaning of his life from God and the order in the world He made.

---

9   From the Greek term *mimos*, "imitator." Man imitates, or follows, the pattern set forth by the Maker.

When man lacks the sense of being created, he experiences dysphoria: he is alone in the cosmos, lost and fragmented. In this view of the world, the *poietic*[10] view, man must create his own meaning from the situation in which he finds himself. There is no external order or rules. In fact, to follow any rules or imitate what others do would be the height of inauthenticity. While the philosophical underpinnings for the poietic view have been growing for centuries, only in recent generations have they become widespread. This is enhanced by technological developments that place into our pockets, on our wrists, and over our eyes devices that cast the illusion that reality is malleable. Inside "virtual reality," people, topography, tools, and weapons exist to be grasped, reshaped, abused, or discarded. The Nicene Creed's confession that the Son of God "was made man" no longer seems as consequential to people who believe that the difference between a man and a woman is one of will, not of biology. Human nature is not bound by biology (or any natural law). Instead, it is created by the individual. In such a world, the idea of a Redeemer is not only unnecessary but offensive.

The strong feeling of disconnection between generations, and between Christians and the non-Christian community, is the result of the loss of common assumptions about the nature of the world and man's place in it. The so-called culture wars were not really about abortion, homosexuality, posting the Ten Commandments, or prayer in public schools. They were about whether man makes his own reality or if the world has an external order impressed upon it. In other words, whether man makes or man is made (by a Maker). The Church, living in a culture that has embraced the poietic view, faces tremendous challenges. Christians

---

10 From the Greek term *poiein*, "to make." Man makes his own meaning and purpose in the world apart from any external standards. For an extended evaluation of these concepts, see Carl Trueman, *The Rise and Triumph of the Modern Self: Cultural Amnesia, Expressive Individualism, and the Road to Sexual Revolution* (Wheaton, IL: Crossway, 2020).

must now live in a world that is moving rapidly away from the idea that reality has any intrinsic meaning. Humanity has no particular purpose (*telos*). By contrast, the task of the Church today is to bring the world's meaning, and man's purpose, back into the minds of people.

Though theologians frequently lay blame for the current situation at the feet of the ancient Gnostics, one can also find the seeds of the present problem in Western medieval theology. In the twelfth century, scholastic theologians fused Aristotelian metaphysics with Christian theology, a project that reached its apex with the intellectual giant Thomas Aquinas. Aquinas and his predecessors used the term *transubstantiation* to give a philosophical explanation for the presence of Christ's body and blood in the bread and wine of the Lord's Supper. Whereas the apostolic age was content to describe this as a mystery, the medieval age—no doubt unintentionally—introduced speculative, extrabiblical notions that regarded the created element of bread becoming an illusion, its substance not joined but replaced by Christ's.[11]

Here is how transubstantiation works: things have *accidents* and *substance*. The accidents are how a thing looks, smells, feels, sounds, and tastes. The substance is the essence of the thing itself; in the case of bread, its "breadness." The theory of transubstantiation is that in the sacrifice of the Mass, the Roman priest (by the power placed in him at ordination) effects a change (*trans*) in the bread's substance so that the accidents of bread remain, but it is no longer bread. The substance is now Christ's body.

With the doctrine of transubstantiation, the philosophical

---

11 The Reformation view reflected in Luther's Small Catechism affirms that both body and bread are truly present in the Lord's Supper (likewise both blood and wine), although how that is remains a mystery. The Sacrament of the Altar "is the true body and blood of our Lord Jesus Christ under the bread and wine, instituted by Christ Himself for us Christians to eat and to drink" (Small Catechism, Sacrament of the Altar, What is the Sacrament of the Altar?).

seeds are thereby sown for a separation of a thing's characteristics from its true nature (or substance). Except for how the change is effected (by the power of the priest), this is profoundly similar to the argument for transgenderism. Transgender ideology claims, for example, that a person's characteristics (biology) can give every appearance of being male, but the true essence (or *substance*) of the person is female. Accident becomes illusion. Like the bread of the Eucharist, the theory claims the human body of the transgender person is a deceitful shadow, while the true person is something vastly different than what the body portrays.

This disconnection from creation leads to identity confusion for everyone. God made the human person to be a constitutive whole, where body and soul (or spirit, mind, or heart) describe different facets or capabilities of an indivisible person. Humans are embodied souls (or ensouled bodies), not souls inhabiting bodies for a time, later to exchange their individual body for some other conveyance the way we may trade in one automobile for another.

Transgenderism is thus the ultimate expression of the conceptual separation of self from body. Defining self as "will" or "desire" moves people away from the reality in which God made them. We do not create the self; we are created. God makes; man is made. It is He who made us, and not we ourselves.

Conclusion

Even the most pious Christian today is affected by the culture and thought patterns that surround us. We subjectively interpret the world and our lives psychologically more than using the objective criteria of creation (science) and the Creator (theology). It is imperative to ground personal, family, and church life in the primary relationship between the Maker and those made. The problems we label psychological are more properly understood as stemming from the cosmic problem of corruption. God's Word calls this "the fear of death," the topic of our next chapter.

REFLECTION QUESTIONS

1. From what do you derive your personal sense of identity?

2. How has the current cultural instability affected you?

3. What is an authentic life?

4. What is your source of truth?

5. How does God describe the first man He made?

6. What are the constitutive parts of a human being?

7. How should we speak about the human person after death?

8. How should we use the phrase "living together"?

9. What kind of dominion was man meant to have?

10. Why did God make man?

CHAPTER 2

THE FEAR OF DEATH

Introduction

In the first chapter, we began to unpack our society's quest to affix blame for world problems in the Marxist language of oppression. This societal notion divides the population into sinners and those sinned against. Those who work to identify the root cause of these social ills through this lens often borrow the Christian language of original sin. From the actual Christian worldview, however, the consequences of the fall of our first parents affect us all. There is no group of people with greater responsibility for the human condition than Adam and Eve (although certainly particular sins are committed by particular people). Original sin is a cosmic problem that requires a divine remedy. This chapter examines the consequences of the fall according to God's Word: pain in childbearing and conflict between woman and man; hostile creation, difficult work, and death; and the loss of God's presence with man. It then explores how human anxiety, mental illness, and grasping for power and possessions all originate in what the Bible calls "the fear of death," which holds humans in bondage (Hebrews 2:15).

Corruption Invades the World

"The day that you eat of it you shall surely die" (Genesis 2:17). The Lord warned the first man of this punishment if he disobeyed God's Word. Death, however, was not instantaneous. Rather, with the first

sin, corruption entered man's body and mind and began destroying him. Corruption entered also into the world, turning it against
man. "The creation was subjected to futility" (Romans 8:20).

At the creation of the woman, our first father, Adam, rejoiced:
"This at last is bone of my bones and flesh of my flesh; she shall be
called Woman, because she was taken out of Man" (Genesis 2:23).
Their existence was unhindered by competition, judgment, or se-
crets: "And the man and his wife were both naked and were not
ashamed" (v. 25). They were unaware of their nakedness. Their natural state was full acceptance. Love was without lust. No thought of
possession entered their minds. The fullness of their being was on
display toward the other. Each was oriented toward the other; each
derived meaning from the word God had spoken and the task He
had given of stewarding His creation.

Curved In on the Self

Immediately upon the transgression of God's command (Genesis 3:1–6), they became self-conscious: "Then the eyes of both
were opened, and they knew that they were naked. And they sewed
fig leaves together and made themselves loincloths" (v. 7). Prior to
the transgression, they were naked and without shame. After, their
nakedness brought shame. They sought to hide from each other.
They were turned inward.

This is the first consequence of the fall, that man is curved in
on himself. To be curved in on yourself is to place self-interest and
self-preservation above all else, regardless of truth or the consequences others will experience. Even after Baptism and regeneration, we continue to be selfish. Baptism forgives the guilt of original sin but does not change its effects. The old Adam still seeks to
overcome the new man. In a lecture on Psalm 25, Martin Luther

put it this way: "If we examine ourselves carefully, therefore, we shall always find in ourselves at least vestiges of the flesh by which we are afflicted with self-interest, obstinate over against the good, and prone to do evil."[12] This self-interest led our first parents to place the blame elsewhere instead of confessing their sin. Adam blamed his wife (and ultimately God, who had given her to be with him). The woman blamed the serpent. Neither took personal responsibility. Neither confessed. Neither pleaded for mercy.

A Dreadful Enemy

The curse God pronounced upon the serpent after he tempted Adam and Eve to sin contains a promise filled with great joy: the Seed of the woman (the Messiah, our Lord Jesus Christ) will crush the serpent's head. This is the work Jesus accomplished as He obeyed His Father's will, both actively (by keeping the Law for us) and passively (by allowing Himself to be punished on the cross for our sin). "The reason the Son of God appeared was to destroy the works of the devil" (1 John 3:8).

In man's life now, prior to the Day of Judgment, however, he has a formidable enemy: "on earth is not his equal."[13] The devil rages against mankind, especially against those who have become disciples of Jesus. By teaching us to say "Our Father," Jesus made us not just His disciples but also His brothers. When the devil could not destroy the Savior, he set out to destroy those who call upon the Savior's name. Revelation 12:17 describes the devil as a dragon who is at war with "the woman," who is "the church, the bride of the exalted Christ":[14] "The dragon became furious with the woman

---

12 Martin Luther, *Luther's Works*, American Edition, vol. 25: *Lectures on Romans*, ed. Hilton C. Oswald (St. Louis: Concordia Publishing House, 1972), 245.

13 Martin Luther, "A Mighty Fortress Is Our God" (*LSB* 656:1).

14 Louis A. Brighton, *Revelation,* Concordia Commentary (St. Louis: Concordia Publishing House, 1999), 339.

and went off to make war on the rest of her offspring, on those who keep the commandments of God and hold to the testimony of Jesus." The devil is at war with the disciples of Jesus. The devil is at war with you. He is your enemy. Of this enemy, you must be constantly on guard. St. Peter says, "Be sober-minded; be watchful. Your adversary the devil prowls around like a roaring lion, seeking someone to devour. Resist him, firm in your faith" (1 Peter 5:8–9). We will discuss how to battle against this dreadful enemy in chapter 11, "Battling Your Demons."

The Woman's Pain

The Lord's curse next turns to the woman: "I will surely multiply your pain in childbearing; in pain you shall bring forth children. Your desire shall be contrary to your husband, but he shall rule over you" (Genesis 3:16). This pain in childbearing is indeed a curse, but it is "a happy and joyful punishment"[15] because it is in harmony with the promise in Genesis 3:15 that a male child of the woman would crush the serpent's head. Why is childbearing mentioned? This pertains to the uniqueness of the woman; she alone can bear a child. Her biological distinctiveness from the man sets her apart for this joyous calling. Yet, in the curse of the fall, this joy turns to pain. While this certainly is a physical pain, the Hebrew term used can also refer to a pain in the mind or emotions,[16] leading some Bible translations to translate it as sorrow.[17]

This is important because the pain women feel as a result of their calling to be mothers is not only experienced in the hardship of pregnancy and the peril of childbirth. Women who have diffi-

---

15 Martin Luther, *Luther's Works*, American Edition, vol. 1: *Lectures on Genesis: Chapters 1–5*, ed. Jaroslav Jan Pelikan, trans. George V. Schick (St. Louis: Concordia Publishing House, 1958), 198.

16 See Ronald B. Allen, "1666 עָצַב," *Theological Wordbook of the Old Testament*, ed. R. Laird Harris, Gleason L. Archer Jr., and Bruce K. Waltke (Chicago: Moody Press, 1999), 687–88.

17 For example, the King James Version, New King James Version, and Wycliffe Bible uses "sorrow" in Genesis 3:16 in place of the second "pain" in the English Standard Version.

culty conceiving may experience a loss comparable to death. Rachel said to Jacob, "Give me children, or I shall die!" (Genesis 30:1). The agony of miscarriage or stillbirth often leads bereft mothers to ponder what they did wrong, how they have offended God, why He hates them, or if their children are damned. The melancholy of shattered maternity, often suffered in secret, is a grief that rarely resolves in this life. Of course, the husband of this barren relationship also agonizes. Like the curse of the man, the curse of the woman is specific but is to some degree shared in sympathy by the opposite sex.

Every year at the March for Life in Washington, DC, I see women carrying signs that say "I Regret My Abortion." The women who realize what they have done carry a torment few others could comprehend. Often driven to abortion while in seemingly hopeless situations, they realize a deeper hopelessness as they discover that the solution is more wretched than the problem. It is imperative that the church speak unequivocally to the evils of abortion and speak just as confidently about the forgiveness found in Jesus, who took on flesh in Mary's womb to remedy every evil and to effect full and free absolution to grieving mothers.

The second part of Eve's curse was having a conflicted relationship with her husband. The ESV does well in rendering this as "Your desire shall be contrary to your husband." Other translations (e.g., NKJV, NIV) render it as a desire *for* her husband. This makes what follows—that the man rules over her—seem like a betrayal: the woman desires her husband, but he responds with domineering abuse. The term *desire* used here by the Lord is in the context of how sin has damaged her nature; it is a desire to control the man. No longer were they "naked and were not ashamed" (Genesis 2:25), open and guileless; now there is competition and a struggle.

Compare the same language used in Genesis 4, where the Lord chastises Cain, who is angry after the controversy with Abel about worship and sacrifice (see Genesis 4:3–5). The Lord says to Cain, "If you do not do well, sin is crouching at the door. Its *desire* is contrary to you, but you must *rule* over it" (Genesis 4:7, emphasis added). Sin is personified as a predator lying in wait for its prey. Its desire is not loving; it is intent on destruction. The man of God is exhorted to do battle with it ("rule over it").

Because of the corruption of human nature, this same battle now erupts between the woman and her husband. She desires to control and enslave her husband, and he in turn subdues her with aggressive strength. The joy Adam expressed upon beholding his newly fashioned wife was short-lived. Ever since, husbands and wives have had to struggle with these tensions inherent in their fallen nature.

The Man's Labor

As the woman's curse affects the man in their warring relationship, so the man's curse in hard labor and death also applies to the woman. To the man, the Lord said, "Cursed is the ground because of you; in pain you shall eat of it all the days of your life; thorns and thistles it shall bring forth for you; and you shall eat the plants of the field. By the sweat of your face you shall eat bread, till you return to the ground, for out of it you were taken; for you are dust, and to dust you shall return" (Genesis 3:17–19). While man had a task to perform from the beginning—stewarding the world in its development and raising children to fill the earth—such work was not filled with pain. The garden God made provided the food man needed. It was there for the taking—or it would be better to say it was there for the receiving, with thanksgiving to the Creator.

The earth was created to be supportive of mankind, providing both sustenance and beauty. Then corruption entered.

The earth became hostile to man. It would yield its produce with reluctance. Thorns—which one day would crown the Lord Jesus as He became king of the curse and the representative of all mankind—now ensnared the earth's fruit. Deprived of the perfect food of Eden, man must now make bread. Tilling the earth, planting grain, protecting the field, harvesting, grinding the grain into flour, gathering and mixing other ingredients, kneading, and baking: a loaf of bread would only come through long months of toil and sweat. And the earth he worked would be the place of his return. Man returns to the dust—the very dust the serpent eats (v. 14).

Exile

Unspoken, yet evident in the curse of the fall, is the loss of access to God's presence. Even before His incarnation, the Second Person of the Trinity appeared in the form of a man and came among our first parents. They recognized the sound of His walking and knew the customary time of His appearing (Genesis 3:8). We can only speculate what wonders His presence must have brought. As He cared for them like a father, did God teach them language and other knowledge of the created world?

With terrible dread, God now drives them out of their perfect home, posting spirit soldiers at the entrance and a rotating sword of fire to bar their return. Man's existence since has been of a people bereft of a home. The particular experience of exile and slavery, such as the Jews experienced in Egypt and Babylon, are examples of the larger exile of the entire human race. Man's desire to return to a golden age, or progress toward a utopia, reflect the longing deep in the heart of mankind for the lost Eden. The church's song reflects this longing to return home, as in this hymn for the Holy Spirit's help:

That He may defend us when life is ending
And from exile home we are wending.
Lord, have mercy![18]

The Fear of Death

When the Holy Scriptures speak of the "fear of death" (Hebrews 2:15), they are indicating a far deeper problem than fixating on the manner of one's demise. Some people are afraid to fly on airplanes, while others may take extreme, even irrational, precautions against a spreading virus. But the biblical fear of death has more to do with the underlying anxiety that besets us when we realize that the world we experience is temporal. Some hoarders hoard in an attempt to hold onto a past that has already slipped away. How difficult it is to part with clothes that the children have outgrown! Toys, art projects, and any memento kept is clinging to a stage of childhood that will not return.

Called to the scene of a traffic accident by an involved parishioner, I heard a person crying repeatedly, "My beautiful car! My beautiful car!" Totaled, it would now be carried away to an automotive grave or wherever mangled metals go. But that beautiful car was always a kind of illusion. Regardless of traffic collisions, every new vehicle eventually meets its first shopping cart, a rock flung up by a speeding semi, or some other object that begins the trajectory toward ultimate obsolescence. We cannot keep it new.

As a baby, my son had exceptionally beautiful skin. Perhaps every parent thinks that. Despite my own experiences with injuries,

18   Martin Luther, "To God the Holy Spirit Let Us Pray" (*LSB* 768:1).

scars, acne, and all the other joys that come with boyhood, I was surprised at the loss I felt when seeing the bloody gash above my son's right eye after a fall. Although the wonderful team at the hospital lovingly stitched him up, my wife and I shared the sadness that his "perfect" face was perfect no more. We know full well that he will die the same as every person, yet this new imperfection brought melancholy. Death is coming, but we do not want to admit that. Every harbinger of it exposes the fear. We cannot keep him "new."

Creation was meant to reflect a deeper reality, pointing us to its Maker and His love. With corruption invading the world, man's life instead is filled with anxiety as he discovers poisoned food and animals turned hostile. The need for shelter from intemperate elements, uncertain harvests, and swarming insects makes creation capricious at best. His thoughts breed disease as he reflects on the antagonism of the world.

Conclusion

Man exists in exile. Those without the knowledge of God seek a paradise of their own making, only to see it become a prison. Christians see the world as made by God but corrupted through the fall of all humanity in our first parents. Every human bears the heavy yoke of this curse from childhood. Besides the consequences of death and fear outlined in this chapter, there is a profound darkness in the human heart of disordered desires. That is the next topic of our study.

REFLECTION QUESTIONS

1. What were the consequences of the fall?

2. In what ways does being "curved in on yourself" harm your neighbors?

3. How should the knowledge that you are "curved in on yourself" shape your prayer and devotional life?

4. Have you struggled with anxiety or anger? How might this be connected to what Hebrews describes as "anxious thought" regarding "the fear of death?

CHAPTER 3

APPETITE FOR DESTRUCTION

Introduction

The rebellion of our first parents was not about fruit. It was about autonomy, self-rule, to be one's own arbiter of the law. But the quest for self-rule did not result in man's liberation. Instead, he found himself enslaved to his own desires. What is worse, those desires were not oriented toward his own good. Man now craves the very things that will destroy him. He is like a dehydrated man thirsty for poison. In this chapter, we will examine the corruption of the human heart, the distinction between venial and mortal sin (it's not what you think!), and what it means to be happy.

Man in Chains

Philosopher Jean Jacques Rousseau (1712–78) famously opened his work *The Social Contract* by writing that "man is born free; and everywhere he is in chains." The Scriptures describe man's condition as just the opposite: man is born in chains (bondage to corruption), yet everywhere thinks he is free. The diabolical appeal to our first parents had its root in autonomy—to be a law unto oneself, the arbiter of what is good and evil apart from the Word of God.

To understand yourself, you need to be aware of the crucible in which you were formed. The postmodern worldview permeates our culture. It's not necessary that you study the philosophical underpinnings of postmodernism, but it is extremely helpful to know the basics. Postmodernists are deeply skeptical that one can know objective truth. Truth claims, they say, are cultural constructs. Thus, what you stream on your tablet, experience in the classroom, or hear through your earbuds is likely to be founded in a rejection of not just Christianity but also shared morality or a common conception of what is good, true, and beautiful.

Postmodernism believes the societal structure in which we live is inherently evil, shaped by hierarchical power systems.[19] In the riotous summer of 2020, following the killing of George Floyd, the burning of police departments and government buildings was no mere response to perceived injustices. The street fighters saw themselves as igniting a revolution against the fundamentally corrupt system of Western government, law, and morality.[20]

While the particular philosophical movement driving the street fighters is only a few centuries old, its roots are ancient. The action of our first parents was no mere lust for fruit. They turned away from the divinely established hierarchy: God speaks, man hears and responds with grateful obedience. The first man and his wife sought to level the playing field by acquiring God's knowledge independently of Him: "When you eat of it your eyes will be opened, and you will be like God, knowing good and evil" (Genesis 3:5).

Now man determines good and evil apart from God. Or such is what he thinks. In truth, man is inclined toward evil. The chapters in Genesis following the fall of our first parents detail a growing degeneracy in the world. But the increasing debasement was not

---

19   See, e.g., Helen Pluckrose and James A. Lindsay, *Cynical Theories: How Activist Scholarship Made Everything about Race, Gender, and Identity—and Why This Harms Everybody* (Durham, NC: Pitchstone Publishing, 2020).

20   See Andy Ngo, *Unmasked: Inside Antifa's Radical Plan to Destroy Democracy* (New York: Center Street, 2021).

merely one of behavior. It was in man's mind and heart: "The LORD saw that the wickedness of man was great in the earth, and that every intention of the thoughts of his heart was only evil continually" (Genesis 6:5). Notice how comprehensive this is. Not some or most intentions, but every one of them. Not partly evil or mostly evil, but only evil. Not some of the time or most of the time, but continually.

That verse precipitates the destruction of the world by the great flood. Only eight people were preserved through that deluge: Noah and his family. Yet their salvation was not through a righteousness of their own. Noah found favor—grace[21]—in the Lord's eyes (see Genesis 6:8). Noah had no claim to make on God because he was different from other men; his salvation rested in God's pity, love, and mercy. This was evident in the repetition of the declaration regarding the comprehensive corruption of man's nature after the flood: "And when the LORD smelled the pleasing aroma [of Noah's sacrifice], the LORD said in His heart, 'I will never again curse the ground because of man, for the intention of man's heart is evil from his youth[22]'" (Genesis 8:21).

What the Bible teaches from the earliest chapters is that man's nature now is enslaved by evil desires. Two natural objections to this immediately suggest themselves: the Bible describes certain men as righteous, and we have friends or relatives whom we would describe as good. How then can it be that everyone is enslaved to evil desires?

Here it is necessary to distinguish between righteousness before men (civil righteousness) and righteousness before God. When it comes to civil righteousness, people are capable of performing, and

---

21 חֵן. See *TWOT* Number 694a. *Theological Wordbook of the Old Testament*, ed. R. Laird Harris, Gleason L. Archer Jr., and Bruce K. Waltke (Chicago: Moody Press, 1999).

22 *Youth* is more comprehensive in Hebrew (נְעוּרִים) in that it includes infants and very young children, e.g., the infant Moses (Exodus 2:6) and the newborn child of Bathsheba (2 Samuel 12:16).

indeed do perform, good works, such as paying their taxes, driving according to the rules of the road, transacting their business honestly and honorably, caring for their children, and looking out for their neighbors. These people are good—as men judge goodness.

God, however, looks at the heart. Much of the good that men do, they do out of self-interest. Obedience to the civil law means avoiding penalties such as fines, loss of property, and imprisonment. Dishonorable behavior leads to a loss of reputation and opportunities for advancement. On a very practical level, my wife is happy (on the rare occasion) when I help clean up the kitchen. My life is improved when she is happy. Therefore, I don't truly help her for her sake; I help her for mine. Can a man do even one truly good act in all his life? Not in, of, or by himself. The holy prophet Jeremiah even tells us that we cannot comprehend the depth of our depravity: "The heart is deceitful above all things, and desperately sick; who can understand it?" (Jeremiah 17:9). Every good thing in the world we take and ruin. The reformer Martin Luther put it this way in his lectures on Romans:

> Our nature has been so deeply curved in upon itself because of the viciousness of original sin that it . . . turns the finest gifts of God in upon itself and enjoys them . . . , indeed, it even uses God Himself to achieve these aims, but it also seems to be ignorant of this very fact, that in acting so iniquitously, so perversely, and in such a depraved way, it is even seeking God for its own sake.[23]

Thus, after the primordial chapters, the Scriptures continue to describe man's nature as altogether ruined. David's prayer of

23   Martin Luther, *Luther's Works*, American Edition, vol. 25: *Lectures on Romans*, ed. Hilton C. Oswald (St. Louis: Concordia Publishing House, 1972), 291.

confession after his sin with Bathsheba shows that man's corruption is inherited: "Behold, I was brought forth in iniquity, and in sin did my mother conceive me" (Psalm 51:5). "Brought forth" refers to the agonizing writhing of childbirth; "iniquity" refers to an act of moral wrongdoing. Hebrew poetry, such as is found in the psalms, often works by parallel speech. For example, a psalm will have a statement in the first half of a verse, and then say the same thing using different terms in the second half. A variation on this is that the original statement will be intensified. Psalm 51:5 is an excellent example of this. After David says that at the time of his birth, he was committing moral wrongs, he goes on to say that at the time of his conception, he had already fallen short of what God intended for him. That's a nuance of the term *sin*; it's not so much about an action as it is a failure to act correctly. The common definition of *sin* is helpful here: "to miss the mark." Think of a basketball player shooting the ball. If it's an airball, not going in the hoop, then it's a sin: the player missed the mark. Each moment that we fail to be and do what God meant for us is another moment in sin. This way of thinking means that sin is more than a list of the bad things we have done; sin is all the ways we have not been what God meant for us to be. This situation exists from the moment of each person's conception. Every child born, from our first parents on, is in this state of fallenness, of lacking what God meant for a human person to be.

Inherited Contagion

This condition is frequently called *original sin*. However, that term is misleading, since *original* can mean "the first of something." Examples of this would be "The original building was located downtown" or "The original recipe called for butter instead of margarine." But *original sin* is not talking about the first sin our first parents committed. It means the sin we are born with, the sin we have already in our origins when we originate from our parents. Even this can be a little confusing since people often think that being born with sin means being born with guilt that properly belongs to another. In other words, Why should a child be blamed for what the parents did? Certain passages of Scripture can be cited to reject that very idea, such as Ezekiel 18:20, "The soul who sins shall die. The son shall not suffer for the iniquity of the father, nor the father suffer for the iniquity of the son. The righteousness of the righteous shall be upon himself, and the wickedness of the wicked shall be upon himself."

Because the term is so easily confused, the clearest theologians of the Reformation used terms like *inherited sin* and *inherited contagion*. By thinking of the innate flaw of each human person as a contagion (disease), we can more easily see the situation. We have inherited a condition from our parents, similar to other characteristics that we readily understand are hereditary. What is the contagion we have inherited? One word best captures the fullness of the malady: *corruption*.

Corruption

Corruption is an excellent term for man's condition because it has such a broad meaning. It applies to material destruction: metal rusts, milk spoils, cheese grows moldy, termites devour buildings, and corpses decay. Corruption is death. That is man's bodily condition. The beauty of God's intention is evident in youth, but quickly man stumbles and wrinkles as gravity pulls him down toward his eventual grave. Isaiah describes it as a flower, beautiful only for a short time: "All flesh is grass, and all its beauty is like the flower of the field. The grass withers, the flower fades when the breath of the LORD blows on it; surely the people are grass" (Isaiah 40:6–7). The same image is found in the Psalm of Moses, which describes the limits on man's life and the swiftness of our demise: "All our days pass away under Your wrath; we bring our years to an end like a sigh. The years of our life are seventy, or even by reason of strength eighty; yet their span is but toil and trouble; they are soon gone, and we fly away" (Psalm 90:9–10). Each person is born into this corruption; no one can stave off death.

Another kind of corruption we are quite familiar with is the kind we find everywhere in human society. This corruption includes politicians enriched by shady deals, government bureaucrats abusing power, college admissions slots sold to the highest bidder, law enforcement spying on politicians, and sometimes, getting away with murder. Everyone deplores corruption when it is on "the other team." But the Scriptures teach us that every human person is corrupt, that is, deceitful, dishonorable, and untrustworthy. David writes, "They are corrupt, they do abominable deeds; there is none who does good. The LORD looks down from heaven on the children of man, to see if there are any who understand, who seek after God. They have all turned aside; together they have become corrupt; there is none who does good, not even one" (Psalm 14:1–3). We are born this way: corrupt in heart and mind, corrupt in body.

Disordered Desire

The corruption in our heart and mind is called *concupiscence.* This Latin term is often translated into English as *lust*. However, I think that is unhelpful, as lust in common usage usually means sexual desire. Concupiscence includes sexual desire but is much more than that. Concupiscence is the intense desire to do what is contrary to the will of God. I think *disordered desire* best explains the problem in our own heart, mind, and will.

Desires, of course, are often quite natural and good. The body uses the signals of desire to let us know what is needed. After a salty meal, we crave water. When we work in the hot sun, we cry out for shade or a cool mist to bring our temperature down. A long, challenging day at work leaves us desiring rest and sleep.

But in the corruption of the human will, every desire becomes disordered. Curved in on ourselves, we abuse the gifts God has given. So the desire for food can overwhelm a person to the point of eating too much unhealthy food. The natural desire for sleep leads some to rest too much, and they become indolent. A physician prescribes powerful drugs to ease pain, but the patient becomes addicted and the medicine becomes a destructive poison.

How can we distinguish rightly ordered desire from disordered desire? The Decalogue.[24] The Law is good, and it shows what is pleasing to God. While the Law certainly has a negative function in exposing sin, this is not its only function. The theological phrase *Lex semper accusat* ("The Law always accuses") in practice sometimes is regarded as *Lex sola accusat* ("The Law *only* accuses"). But the Law also serves as a guide, showing us what good works please God and what desires affirm God and His creation. To bring our desires into line with God's original intention for mankind, we must affirm the goodness of God's moral code along with our innate will to reject it—and beware of theological attempts to subvert God's Word through subtle incursions of antinomianism.[25]

---

24 Another way to say the Ten Commandments.
25 Antinomianism is the teaching that God's Law places no requirements on the life of the Christian since he is saved by grace. This error continues in practical ways to the present day through "Gospel reductionism." See Scott Murray, *Law, Life, and the Living God: The Third Use of the Law in Modern American Lutheranism* (St. Louis: Concordia Publishing House, 2001).

Disconnected from the Decalogue, or any higher will or purpose, the individual declares that his human will is sovereign. In theological terms, the human will replaces God as the object of worship. Man grasps for what he desires, the only constraint being societal—what he can get away with. This reveals itself especially in the area of sexual relations.

Fertility and Fecundophobia

God made us for sexual relations. "Be fruitful and multiply" (Genesis 1:28) is a blessed ordinance that continues to the end of the world. The traditional marriage rite goes so far as to say it is good to enjoy it: "Marriage was also ordained so that man and woman may find delight in one another."[26] This extraordinary gift, under the corrupting influence of sin, becomes a powerful force, enslaving people to its pursuit outside of the arena for which God intended it: holy matrimony. Reformation teaching was extremely clear that marriage's purpose is procreation:

> The rest of the populace is more wicked than even the heathen themselves. For most married people do not desire offspring. Indeed, they turn away from it and consider it better to live without children, because they are poor and do not have the means with which to support a household. But this is especially true of those who are devoted to idleness and laziness and shun the sweat and the toil of marriage. But the purpose of marriage is not to have pleasure and to be idle but to procreate and bring up children, to support a household. This, of course, is a huge burden full of great cares and toils. But you have been created by

---

26   *LSB*, p. 275.

God to be a husband or a wife and that you may learn to bear these troubles. Those who have no love for children are swine, stocks, and logs unworthy of being called men or women; for they despise the blessing of God, the Creator and Author of marriage.[27]

Despising procreation is not a new problem. What is new, however, are the easy methods and cultural approval to put asunder what God has joined together: sex and babies. Today, fertility has been severed from sex by contraception. Couples who want children are now said to be "trying." Such language is possible only in an age of easily accessible contraception and abortion on demand. Sex, intended for the procreation of children, has become completely disconnected from its intended purpose to the point that families with more than two or three children are ridiculed. Even as birthrates in America and Europe plummet, the rejection of children only becomes more established in our culture.

Should we really be surprised that in the decades since the popularization of contraception (literally "against conception"), humanity has gone from subverting the intention of the sexual organs to open rebellion against those organs themselves? The very notion of "sex change" (now euphemistically called "gender reassignment surgery" or even "gender affirmation") by destroying the natural function of the body, embraces a rebellion against the Author of life that Onan could not have imagined.[28] The natural desire given by God, both for joy in marriage and to be fruitful and multiply, has become deeply disordered.

---

27 Martin Luther, *Luther's Works*, American Edition, vol. 5, *Lectures on Genesis Chapters 26–30*, ed. Jaroslav Pelican and Walter A. Hansen, trans. George V. Schick and Paul D. Pahl (St. Louis: Concordia Publishing House, 1968), 363.

28 After the death of Judah's son Er, Onan was required to have conjugal relations with Er's wife, Tamar, so that she might bear a child. But Onan wasted his semen on the ground, preventing Tamar from becoming pregnant. This account in Scripture (Genesis 38:1–11) is frequently cited in theological discussions around the purpose of marriage and issues related to fertility and contraception.

Because this desire is so powerful, one's personal predilections become the essence of self-identity.

Disordered desires plague our every moment, waking and even sleeping. Are they sin? Yes. But here we must make a distinction between the sinful *nature* and sinful *actions*. Before we can do that, however, we must deal with a challenge in understanding the term *nature*.

A Word about Nature

Christian teaching and liturgy frequently use the word *nature* to refer to our tendencies. A common confession of sins uses the term this way, acknowledging the inherited contagion of disordered desires (i.e., original sin): "Most merciful God, we confess that we are *by nature* sinful and unclean. We have sinned against You in thought, word, and deed, by what we have done and by what we have left undone."[29] The problem comes when we think about nature in the stricter sense, as the essence of a creature. I am a human being, not a platypus. A platypus has a different nature from a human being, or a penguin, porpoise, or panda bear. Each of these different creatures was made by God. And God declared all of them *good*.[30]

To say, then, that something is wrong with the nature of a human being comes dangerously close to making God a creator of evil. When we speak in a narrow way about the essence of humanity, we must say that nature is good because God made it. In its essence, human nature is good, but the contagion brought in by the sin of our first parents has made it defective.

Remember, then, that when Christians confess that they are by nature sinful, they are not saying that God made people for evil

29   *LSB*, p. 151, emphasis added.
30   See Genesis 1:21, 24, 31.

purposes; they are saying that men now have a proclivity to wickedness. They are oriented against God's Word and will. Scripture calls this impulse "the old man."[31] Luther put it this way: "The term 'old man' describes what kind of person is born of Adam, not according to his nature but according to the defect of his nature. For his nature is good, but the defect is evil."[32] This defect means that man apart from the Holy Spirit loves the disordered desires and cannot of his own volition turn them toward the good.

The Sin We Are and the Sin We Do

It is helpful, therefore, to distinguish between two categories of sin: *inherited* (or original) sin and *actual* sin. Inherited sin is truly sin. *Actual* here doesn't mean "real" or "true," but finds its root in the word *action*. Men are born with the inherited impulse to sin (concupiscence); acting on that impulse is called *actual sin*. I have developed my own terms for this to make it easier to understand: there is the sin that we are, and the sin that we do. The inherited impulse to sin, along with the corruption of the body, is *the sin that we are*, while our particular transgressions and failures are *the sins that we do*.

What is critical to remember is that no one has greater or less guilt, or dignity, from birth. Every one of us is born this way, born with the inherited contagion, the orientation against God's Law. This is imperative for a correct understanding of controverted issues such as sexual orientation, gender identity, race, eugenics, intellectual disabilities, and other issues of human nature and human rights in twenty-first-century Western society.

---

31   "Do not lie to one another, seeing that you have put off the old self with its practices" (Colossians 3:9). The ESV here translates *anthrōpon* (man, human being) as "self." Other translations, such as the New King James, render the phrase "old man."

32   Martin Luther, *Luther's Works*, American Edition, vol. 25: *Lectures on Romans*, ed. Hilton C. Oswald (St. Louis: Concordia Publishing House, 1972), 313.

While everyone is born with the same inherited contagion, we can distinguish between different types of sins that people commit, particularly the sins of the regenerate.[33] Because the sinful nature—that inherited impulse to sin and reject God's Law—is always raging within us, we are tempted a thousand times a day, even every moment of our lives, to reject God's will for us and succumb to our unholy instincts. When these sins are done reflexively, without consideration or contemplation, they are called *venial sins* (as distinguished from *mortal sins*). (Note: the Roman Church uses the categories of mortal and venial sins in a very different way.)[34] Venial sins are those done out of weakness, thus they are sometimes called sins of impulse or "daily sins." Mortal sins, by contrast, are sins done with consideration, in the full knowledge that it is contrary to God's Law.

A common myth is that committing a single mortal sin results in irrevocable exclusion from the kingdom of God; in other words, it is unforgivable. This is not, however, what is meant by mortal sin. To be mortal is to be subject to death. As an adjective—here modifying *sin*—the term *mortal* means lethal, deadly, killing. Mortal sins affect the soul in such a way that trust in Christ's righteousness is damaged. It is not the particular thing done or omitted that destroys faith; rather, it is the willful rejection of God's Word. When a man purposefully, deliberately rebels against God's will (the Law), he denies the truth and asserts independence from God. The injury done to the soul is severe. It is possible that the person is no longer a Christian (although only God can see the heart and know this for certain). If not, the mortal sin has certainly harmed the

---

33 *Regeneration* is the work of the Holy Spirit in bringing a person from spiritual death to life. The *regenerate* person has been born from above (or, born again) by the Means of Grace, such as Baptism (see John 3:1–5; Titus 3:4–7), along with the Word and the Lord's Supper (see AC V and XIII).

34 For a thorough understanding of the distinction between mortal and venial sin from an orthodox Reformation perspective, see Martin Chemnitz, *Loci Theologici* (St. Louis: Concordia Publishing House, 1989), 667–83.

person in such a way that he is closer to turning entirely away from Jesus, whose disciple he was made in Holy Baptism. Confession is necessary.

Scripture helps us understand the distinction between venial and mortal sin. "Who can discern his errors? Declare me innocent from hidden faults. Keep back your servant also from presumptuous sins; let them not have dominion over me! Then I shall be blameless, and innocent of great transgression" (Psalm 19:12–13). The idea of *venial sin* captures the idea of an error or mistake; the faults are hidden from the one who has them. This passage was significant in the Reformation debates about the necessity of confessing every single sin, as the medieval Roman Church required. It is impossible to know all of our sins.[35] Nevertheless, progress in the Christian life will entail seeing with greater clarity the depth of our sin and the horror of our thoroughgoing corruption.

By contrast, *mortal sin* is a sin of presumption: it may be the presumption that there is no punishment for sin or the presumption that one can willfully defy the Law of God and still receive grace. "Are we to continue in sin that grace may abound? By no means!" (Romans 6:1–2). Such a sin the psalm calls the "great transgression." It is great not simply because of the outward severity but also because the sin has taken ownership of the person. Remember how we saw in the previous chapter that Cain was exhorted to "rule over" his sinful desires (Genesis 4:7)? When the presumptuous sin is committed, concupiscence now rules over the man. David, therefore, prays about "presumptuous sins," "Let them not have dominion over me!" (Psalm 19:13).

What can we learn from this distinction between venial and

---

35 "Our churches teach that private Absolution should be retained in the churches, although listing all sins is not necessary for Confession. For, according to the Psalm, it is impossible. 'Who can discern his errors?'" (AC XI).

mortal sins? First, since even the sins of weakness and impulse are truly sin, we cannot trust our desires. Our own inclinations are at war with God and the new man born again through water and the Word. This truth would have been very helpful to me had I fully understood it earlier in my life.

While attending college in Boston, I lived in a house in Cambridge, Massachusetts, run by a very large, prominent Evangelical church. There, I was taught a theology that emphasized personal piety and freedom from sin. At the time, utterly ignorant of the history of Methodism—a movement founded by John and Charles Wesley that seeks complete perfection in the Christian life—I set forth in a notebook my own methods for "complete sanctification." I intended to do a certain number of actions each day (such as Bible reading and prayer) and address areas of my life that needed improvement (talk less, avert my eyes from attractive women, be charitable to the beggars on the street). The excitement of becoming a perfect person, free from sin, soon turned into frustration. I had more sin than I realized.

As a music student, I knew the secret to success: practice. The best musicians were the ones who took whatever innate talent they had and hauled it into the practice room. That's what I needed to do in my spiritual life. The lists grew longer. I became more miserable. The advice from Evangelical pastors was to try harder. I began wondering if I was a Christian at all.

It's no "tower experience,"[36] but I remember the day distinctly. I was walking through the Cambridge Common, across the street from Harvard University, my thoughts occupied with how I could rid myself of my sins. I heard in my mind (it was a memory, but the

---

36 Luther credits his "discovery" of the Gospel (which was really the result of years of prayer and study of Holy Scripture) to a moment in the tower of his monastery while meditating on promises of God's righteousness in Romans. This is called his "tower experience."

Holy Spirit can work through those too) the voice of my childhood pastor, the sainted Roy Karner, saying to the congregation after the confession of sins, "Almighty God in His mercy has given His Son to die for you and for His sake forgives you all your sins. As a called and ordained servant of the Word I therefore forgive you all your sins in the name of the Father and of the + Son and of the Holy Spirit."[37]

All my sins. Forgiven. What I could not do, Jesus had already done.

The notebook was not useless, but the title needed to change. A better title would have been "The Life of the Justified." I still needed to have a disciplined life of prayer and Scripture reading (and, I learned later, of confession of sins and reception of the Lord's Supper). I still needed to work on my sinful habits. But the power for any of this was founded in the power of Christ's forgiveness and continued in the Holy Spirit's work of sanctification.

The reason I tell of this is to show how a failure to understand the power of concupiscence in our lives will lead to self-justification or self-loathing. My flesh is weak. That will never be entirely tamed in this life. But I am forgiven for this by what Jesus has done. As long as I am in this flesh, I will always need help, grace, and the comfort of the Gospel. As Melanchthon quoted St. Ambrose about the Lord's Supper, "Because I always sin, I always need to take the medicine."[38]

The Enemy Within

Our sin cannot simply be blamed on the devil or external temptations. Your most dangerous enemy is the one inside of you, urging you to satisfy your own desires. Every desire beyond what

37   *Lutheran Worship* (St. Louis: Concordia Publishing House, 1982), 158.
38   AC XXIV 33.

is necessary gives power to death—power that Christ has already stripped from death. The things that are necessary, such as air, water, protection from extreme heat and cold, and nourishment equivalent to our body's need for energy—these natural desires can and should be met. All of our thinking that leads us to sadness and anger, lust and greed, the desire for revenge, the desire to quit—it all comes from giving death power it doesn't have. We are angry and sad, we rage or give up, because it seems as though everything is out of control, that nothing will turn out as we hope. When we know that the one hope, the great hope for the renewal of the world, has already begun in the resurrection of Jesus and has been promised to us in the gift of the Holy Spirit, then no disappointment, no trouble, no loss can overwhelm us. These sufferings, be they ever so great, are like brief pricks of a needle when we get a shot or our blood drawn. Although unpleasant, we know it is but for a moment, and even the pain is working for our good. The hope of the resurrection made the first Christians ready to endure any suffering, even martyrdom. Because everything had changed with the change of Jesus from dead to resurrected.

Your desires are dangerous because they direct you away from what God gives toward what God has withheld. Indulging the desires to which God has said no declares God to be a liar, to not have our best interests at heart. Indulging your desires is an act of rebellion against your Creator.

When God made you, He oriented you toward the good. Now, you are born hardened against God's goodness. In the Gospels, after Jesus teaches that divorce is contrary to the will of God, His detractors try to entrap Him with a question about Old Testament provisions for divorce. In Jesus' response, He specifically notes that man's heart has changed from its original created state. "Because of your hardness of heart Moses allowed you to divorce your wives, but from the beginning it was not so. And I say to you: whoever divorces his wife, except for sexual immorality, and marries another, commits adultery" (Matthew 19:8–9). Man's general hardness of heart both angers and grieves Jesus (see Mark 3:5). It is a frequent cause for His rebuke (e.g., Mark 6:52; 16:14). In the Old Testament, Pharaoh hardened his heart against the Word of God (e.g., Exodus 7:13), but so did the Israelites (Psalm 95:8).

This hardness of heart is our natural condition, and we are continually inclined to return to it. It takes a supernatural act to change the way we were born. This issue was a conflict in the Reformation controversy over the nature of man's will and how a person can be saved. The Roman Catholic Church rejected, and still rejects, the full impact of the bondage of man's will. Philip Melanchthon, the sixteenth-century reformer who issued the decisive rebuttal to the Roman rejection of the Gospel at the Diet of Augsburg (1530), wrote, "Human nature is far too weak to resist the devil by its own powers. He holds as captive everyone who has not been freed through faith. There is need for Christ's power against the devil."[39]

Natural Law and Unnatural Worldviews

While the history of human civilization has had varying degrees of order and chaos at different times, there have generally been overarching social structures holding basic moral standards in place. In recent centuries, however, human society has begun to be unmoored from even the most basic truths of natural law, such as what differentiates a man from a woman. The details of that will be addressed in future chapters. In this next section, we will look at the worldview that enables people now to think in such ways that

---

39   Apology of the Augsburg Confession V 17–18.

were unthinkable to previous civilizations. Philosopher Alasdair Macintyre calls this new way of thinking emotivism.[40]

In chapter 1, we discussed the difference between the *mimetic* and *poietic* worldviews. For a person shaped by the mimetic view, responsibility, duty, and the objective law (for Christians, this includes the Ten Commandments) will be foremost in framing his actions. Thus, a man with a wife is a husband, and he lives out his life doing what husbands do. Toward his children, he is a father, and he does what fathers do. He may be a carpenter, a teacher, a lawyer, a physician—and in those vocations, he performs according to those standards and lives within those hierarchies. He does not seek for himself different identities or create for himself his own meaning. The purpose of his life is to live in the light of the *Torah*, the declaration of God informing him what is good. For such a man, it is unthinkable that he should be a wife or dress as a woman. It is not what he was made to be; it is not how the world is structured.

In the poietic world, as we saw in chapter 1, a person creates his own reality, changing the structure of society and nature. The first such poietic action was when our first parents stepped outside their sphere, calling God a liar and seizing the fruit He had forbidden. They sought divine knowledge apart from the divine gift.

Children today are often asked, "What do you want to be when you grow up?" The implication is that you can be whatever you want. As a child, I wanted to be the catcher for the Minnesota Twins (among other unlikely aspirations). It turns out I needed to be able to hit a curveball if I wanted to go beyond Babe Ruth League, never mind the majors. With harder work, I could have improved, although the natural skill simply wasn't there. Generally,

---

40   See Alasdair MacIntyre, *After Virtue: A Study in Moral Theory*, 3rd ed. (Notre Dame, IN: University of Notre Dame Press, 2007).

a combination of natural skill, hard work, and the right background and opportunity are needed to succeed in something highly specialized.

Behind the question "What do you want to be?" now lies something more sinister: the notion that you can alter the givenness of your being. For a man to simply declare he is a woman, and have others not regard him as insane, is only possible in a poietic society, where natural law, science, and the Word of God all give way to an individual's will. Whatever makes the individual happy is, in a society bereft of God, the only thing worth pursuing.

The Pursuit of Happiness

The American mind has been shaped by, among other things, the values of our core documents. In the Declaration of Independence, Thomas Jefferson wrote that the pursuit of happiness is an inalienable right. Yet Jefferson doubtless defined happiness in the manner of the ancient Greek philosophers, and so intended quite a different meaning than today's idea of happiness. Happiness in this classical sense involves freedom from attachments—what we are calling in this book "the passions." This sort of happiness rises above immediate satisfaction to what will prove beneficial in the long run. Thus, indulging in alcohol or rich food may be quite appealing in the moment, but the indulgence may stand in the way of true happiness when the consequences of such eating or drinking come due. Pursuing happiness, therefore, has moral and societal components and is not equivalent to temporary satiety.

Happiness as a modern value, by contrast, is to feel free of constraint or any unpleasantness. Taken to its conclusion, happiness as the pursuit of personal pleasure will be antithetical to happiness in the classical sense. Consider the case of a husband and wife in a struggling marriage. Those devoted to the pursuit of happiness in the classical sense will strive for harmony in the relationship. Sacrifice, perseverance, compromise, and love as self-giving will all serve the well-being of the marriage in the interest of the higher good. Meanwhile, the modern idea of happiness—freedom from constraint and unpleasantness—will lead to very different efforts and decisions. The dissatisfied spouse will exit the difficult relationship when it no longer serves temporal gratification. To call the separation or divorce a sin will spark hostility toward the offending pastor or friend. It is not enough to call the divorce permissible; it must be recognized by society and even the church as a good and acceptable thing since it leads to happiness for the individual exiting the relationship. "You deserve to be happy," say those liberated from the constraints of external duty or natural law. Such happiness is an immediate psychological state, not the pursuit of what is eternally good. How one feels is the only good.

With happiness (or taste, or desire) as the only good, human nature is reduced to something ephemeral, no more constant than the pixels on a screen. People are plastic, easily remolded or discarded. When the self is the psyche, what is done in the body is merely a matter of utility.

Conclusion

Our desires deceive us. The prescription—and it is lifelong—is to persistently check our desires against the Decalogue and our stations in life. We abide in repentance, imploring God to keep our sins of impulse from becoming willful sins. Happiness is found in embracing God's plan for our life, not in the pursuit of pleasure. Such a life is entirely inconsistent with today's social-media culture, where every moment is an opportunity for self-promotion.

Self-promotion, self-indulgence, self-care—all feed the selfie-beast that aims to turn us all into narcissists.

REFLECTION QUESTIONS

1. What are the basic principles of postmodernism?

2. What does the Bible teach about the nature of man's heart after the fall?

3. What other terms besides *sin* can be used to describe human nature?

4. What happens when man is disconnected from an external law?

5. What is God's purpose for sex?

6. Why are desires dangerous?

7. What are the different understandings of happiness? How has your life been oriented toward one or the other?

CHAPTER 4

SELFIE

Introduction

The disordered desires discussed in the previous chapter find a perfect vehicle for their expression in modern technologies, particularly internet-connected cameras. They are generally called smartphones, but the phone is no longer the principal purpose of these rectangles. Apple introduced the revolutionary iPhone in 2007, with a two-megapixel camera. By 2010, the iPhone 4 sported a front-facing camera in addition to a rear-facing camera. Now you could own a device designed to take pictures of yourself. The addictive quality of electronics was nothing new. But the "selfie" became a new addiction. Taking repeated pictures of yourself would have seemed absurd to previous generations, and manifestly pompous. Setting aside photography enthusiasts, pictures were for capturing events, family, and friends. Photos turned to videos, with younger and younger boys and girls displaying themselves as hyper-sexualized beings desperate for attention. The technology itself isn't the (entire) problem. But its widespread acceptance has transformed how we interact with one another, how children perceive sexuality, and how we present ourselves to the world.

Entranced by the Black Mirror

Walking through the Atlanta airport to catch a connecting flight, I came to one of the long escalators going between the underground tram level and the gate level. As travelers stood on the crammed steps, the multiple escalators going up and down presented a scene of perfect obedience: nearly everyone was staring obediently into their glass rectangles. Unseen were the hits of dopamine they were getting as they scrolled and tapped to get their fix.

If you're on social media, you're almost certainly addicted. The various services (Instagram, Twitter, Facebook, TikTok, YouTube, Snapchat, and whatever else has been added since this writing) have employed modern brain science to keep you staring and searching on their apps, and to return quickly. When your post gets a "like," your brain releases chemicals that make you happy. But it doesn't last, and the more you do it, the more you need. You follow others, some of whom you've never met, in hopes that they'll in turn follow you—and react to what you post. Some services throttle your "likes" to extend your sessions or keep you coming back for more.[41]

There might be some benefits to these services in sharing information and connecting with others. But the drawbacks are extraordinary: rising anxiety, anger, lost time, lost focus, and lost sleep.[42] As Christians, however, we should be concerned about something worse: social media takes the power of concupiscence and amplifies it. The stated goals of social media are not the true goals of the user. Social media accounts are opened to stay connected and informed, but soon, often without thinking, the user's goal becomes self-promotion. We want to be liked. We want others to be dazzled by our wit, stunned at our elegance, and impressed by our busy, picturesque lives. Thus, the user presents a heavily curated self-image—cropped, filtered, and enhanced. As for our enemies, we want

---

41 See Adam Alter, *Irresistible: The Rise of Addictive Technology and the Business of Keeping Us Hooked* (New York: Penguin Press, 2017).

42 For more, see Nicholas Carr, *The Shallows: What the Internet Is Doing to Our Brains* (New York: W. W. Norton and Company, 2011); Cal Newport, *Deep Work: Rules for Focused Success in a Distracted World* (New York: Grand Central Publishing, 2016); and Cal Newport, *Digital Minimalism: Choosing a Focused Life in a Noisy World* (New York: Portfolio/Penguin, 2019).

to see them "owned," or even "slammed," "destroyed," or "silenced." Regardless of how you resolve to behave differently, the environment itself is designed to provoke you to pride and anger, envy and despair. This is not who God made you to be.

Narcissus

I once saw an advertisement for a church with an androgynous figure staring into a pond at its reflection. The invitation to the worship service was presented as an opportunity for self-discovery. At the time, I was stunned by a seemingly positive reference to the Greek myth of Narcissus. I first assumed it was intentional; then I concluded it was out of ignorance. I now see it as unintentionally prophetic.

The myth tells of a handsome warrior, Narcissus, who rejects the nymph Echo's romantic advancements. Nemesis, the goddess of revenge, leads Narcissus to a pool of water, where he becomes obsessed with his image. Realizing his love can never be requited, he dissolves into a flower (in another variation, he commits suicide). Narcissism describes the condition of Narcissus in us, whereby we love ourselves above all. It is embedded in all of us who are, to use a famous Augustine reference, curved in on the self. Narcissism as a particular psychological condition may make sense from a clinical standpoint. From a theological standpoint, however, it is imbued in everyone born of Adam.

Prior to their rebellion, our first parents "were both naked and were not ashamed" (Genesis 2:25). Their attention was not each turned inward but was on God, each other, and the world of which they had been made stewards. In their rebellion, they joined Lucifer in turning their attention to themselves, and so became aware of their nakedness (Genesis 3:7). The whole human race became narcissistic. That is the foundation for the next two scandalous but necessary statements. First, it is my contention that homosexuality is an extreme form of narcissism. *Homo*, Greek for "same," suggests that homosexual desires are a form of love of the self. The original design of mankind is to be oriented toward the other as a form of self-giving. Second, I contend that social media is another form of narcissism. The next section explains this statement further.

Worship My Face

Byzantine-style churches typically have a wall with doors separating the altar from the lay worshipers. On this wall are painted or affixed images of Christ and the saints. This wall is called an *iconostasis*. The images (or icons) are venerated. The worshiper is thus mindful of Christ and the great cloud of witnesses in the saints. Those of the Byzantine tradition worship the face of Christ through the icon. Some churches are further decorated with icons on the surrounding walls and the ceiling. When one worships in a Byzantine-style church, the self is put into the larger context of Christ and His holy ones and should consequently be humbled and driven to repentance. A similar effect is present in the art, statues, and stained glass images in traditional Western churches.

In chapter 1, "The Authentic Self," we observed today's prevailing philosophy: we make ourselves, as opposed to having been made by a Maker. This desire for self-creation combines with the smartphone for self-curation. One's channels on various social media platforms resemble an iconostasis in a Byzantine church, with one image repeatedly appearing: the self in various states of ecstasy and whimsy. While newer American churches are frequently devoid of traditional Christian art (and often theologically opposed to it in principle), the locus of worship has shifted to digital iconostasis. We gaze at our own image, filtered and enhanced. The selfie is our true deity.

Preachers are not immune from this. In fact, they may be more susceptible to it. Standing in the place of God carries the risk of delusion that the preacher is God. The cult of "leadership" drives some men to "never say you're sorry." Many churches once deliberately free of any images now have installed screens. Ostensibly for the display of announcements and lyrics to replace the printed service folder, something new is displayed, larger than life: the face of the preacher. While Christian preaching has historically de-emphasized the personality of the preacher by covering him with vestments and placing him in a pulpit, the modern preacher places himself front and center through digital means. His ministry shifts from personal and liturgical interactions with people to a ministry mediated through screens.

On a vacation Sunday, I once attended a local church head-quartered in Washington, DC, but with "satellite locations" around the suburbs in Maryland and northern Virginia. Seated in a the-ater-style auditorium, complete with cupholders, we enjoyed the brand-name coffee and bagels distributed at the entrance as the band warmed up the crowd. Then came the main attraction: the star preacher appearing by video. It reminded me all at once of Max Headroom, the telescreen from George Orwell's *1984,* and the floor-to-ceiling screens in Ray Bradbury's *Fahrenheit 451.* Would the people who regularly attend that church ever meet the preacher? How did I even know the preacher was real and not computer-generated? It was a step beyond the megachurch ser-vice I once attended where the pastor joked about not knowing the names of the kids invited on stage to receive an award. At least he could see them, and they knew he was a flesh-and-blood human.

With the mediating screen, the pixelated preacher may as well have been from a galaxy far, far away. At least the coffee was good. It was the only real thing I got that Sunday morning.

During the COVID-19 pandemic, many churches resorted to streaming their services on the internet or providing recordings for their congregations. Necessary in some circumstances for a time, it quickly became a significant way of operating for some churches moving beyond the pandemic. Having the pastor detached from the people, mediated through screens, is a substantial change from the church's incarnational ministry, which is centered on human interaction with in-person words and hands that absolve and bless, wash with water, and make personal distribution of sacred food.

Some pastors have left congregations to move into full-time video ministry. Before their carefully curated background, these video preachers gaze into the camera for the latest form of televangelism. While their teaching may be scriptural, their message has subtly shifted from the Word to the icon (not the face of Christ but the face of the video preacher). With selfie-preaching, the face of the preacher becomes the message, potentially wreaking havoc on the messenger's soul in the process.

To see the face of Christ is the longing of the worshiper (see 1 Corinthians 13:12; Revelation 22:4). "Sir, we wish to see Jesus" said the Greeks to Philip (John 12:21). The Aaronic benediction announces the face of YHWH smiling upon His people (Numbers 6:24–26). The pastor dare not replace YHWH's face with his own. Avoid selfie-preachers and disincarnate churches where one cannot have a personal relationship with the pastor.

The Self-Care Trend

Tara Isabella Burton thoughtfully observed the religious

aspects of the modern trend of "Self-Care."[43] Books with titles like *I Love Me More: How to Find Happiness and Success through Self-Love*[44] and *Love Yourself First*[45] reveal the widespread acceptance of an ethic that turns the Scripture's two great commandments on their head.

> "Teacher, which is the great commandment in the Law?" And He [Jesus] said to him, "You shall love the Lord your God with all your heart and with all your soul and with all your mind. This is the great and first commandment. And a second is like it: You shall love your neighbor as yourself. On these two commandments depend all the Law and the Prophets." (Matthew 22:36–40)

Certainly, everyone needs to pay attention to their basic needs for food, sleep, and shelter. But the ubiquitous airline admonition, "Put your own oxygen mask on first before helping others," has been twisted into a license for "self-care," a euphemism for self-love. It is a cultural license for hedonism.

Hēdonē, the Greek word for *pleasure*, is the natural companion of the world's pursuit of happiness and the "authentic" life we have discussed in previous chapters. Christians, by contrast, do not despise pleasure but recognize its danger because of our inherent concupiscence. All truly good pleasures are gifts from God.

Yet we sinners twist this gift of God to fulfill our self-love. The pursuit of pleasure lures many down the broad path leading to destruction. In the parable of the sower, Jesus describes the seed that fell among the thorns as "those who hear, but as they go on

---

43   See *Strange Rites: New Religions for a Godless World* (New York: PublicAffairs, 2020).
44   Jenna Banks (Nashville: Brain Trust Ink, 2022).
45   Amazon sells numerous books by various authors with *Love Yourself First* as part of the title, all published within the last few years.

their way they are choked by the cares and riches and pleasures [hēdonōn] of life, and their fruit does not mature" (Luke 8:14). The apostle Paul notes that the pursuit of pleasure describes the life prior to conversion to be a disciple of Jesus: "For we ourselves were once foolish, disobedient, led astray, slaves to various passions and pleasures [hēdonais], passing our days in malice and envy, hated by others and hating one another" (Titus 3:3). The mention of slavery here shows that hedonism is no mere selfish choice but is the condition of enslavement into which each fallen person is born. People think pleasure will satisfy them, but it instead leaves them empty, with a sensation that life is meaningless and without purpose.

That condition of enslavement leads to conflict:

> What causes quarrels and what causes fights among you? Is it not this, that your *passions* [hēdonōn] are at war within you? You *desire* and do not have, so you murder. You *covet* and cannot obtain, so you fight and quarrel. You do not have, because you do not ask. You ask and do not receive, because you ask wrongly, to spend it on your *passions* [hēdonais]. You adulterous people! Do you not know that friendship with the world is enmity with God? Therefore whoever wishes to be a friend of the world makes himself an enemy of God. (James 4:1–4, emphasis added)

In this remarkable sequence, St. James shows us that the pursuit of pleasure not only produces conflicts with others but also generates an internal civil war: "passions are at war" within the person. Not only does it destroy human relationships but the pursuit of pleasure also separates one from friendship with God. Here hedonism, desire, and covetousness are all joined together to show the state of a person enslaved to his own passions. An important connection is made here to prayer. The person devoted to pleasure may even pray for the satisfaction of his desires, but it reveals his true God: his belly (see Philippians 3:19). This reference to prayer, however, also shows us the way to fight the desire for self-pleasure: petitioning the Lord for a way of escape (1 Corinthians 10:13). When people are habitually fixated on the pursuit of pleasure (e.g., those battling substance addictions or persistent use of pornography), more is required than a simple exhortation to self-control. "Try harder" leads only to pride as long as the will to resist lasts; then self-hatred and disgust after the person falls back into old behaviors. The fight against slavery to pleasure is finally a spiritual battle. Since it is a spiritual battle, the Word of God is our chief weapon, through memorization, recitation, and prayer. (We will discuss this more in chapter 11, "Battling Your Demons.")

Hedonism—the pursuit of pleasure—is finally not a matter of committing this or that sin; it is a matter of how one's life is oriented. Am I walking the narrow way toward the kingdom of God, or am I walking the broad way that leads to destruction (see Matthew 7:13–14)? The myth of autonomy (*auto-nomia* is Greek for "self-law" or "self-rule") is a great deception since, by it, the devil entices you to become instead a slave: "Just as you once presented your members as slaves to impurity and to lawlessness (*anomia*) leading to more lawlessness, so now present your members as slaves to righteousness leading to sanctification. For when you were slaves of sin, you were free in regard to righteousness. But what fruit were you getting at that time from the things of which you are now ashamed? For the end of those things is death" (Romans 6:19–21). Autonomy, the dream of self-rule, ended up being the nightmare of anarchy (lawlessness, *anomia*). Since God's Law is good, and His

Word is life, to follow the way of autonomy/*anomia* disconnects the person from the source of life; he finds only death.

Conclusion

From the emphasis on a psychological view of the world (chapter 1) to becoming turned inward (chapters 2 and 3) to the selfie culture of today's social media, everything around us is a carefully designed prison, preventing us from looking for the face of God. God made the man and the woman to be united in holy marriage, with the sexual union resulting in children and a family. The next step in obscuring man's vision of God is corrupting that sexual union and the purpose of holy marriage. This is the topic of our next chapter.

REFLECTION QUESTIONS

1. In what ways have devices and social media detracted from your life?

2. How does narcissism relate to original sin?

3. What should the pastor's goal be in preaching and worship?

4. How can we distinguish between godly and ungodly pleasures?

5. What does hedonism lead to?

CHAPTER 5

BORN THIS WAY

Introduction

As the front-facing camera technologically fulfilled man's desire to gaze upon himself, the destruction of marriage is the final key to disconnecting sex from love toward neighbor. The selfie culture has a sexual component. It is no surprise that seemingly everyone—from members of congress to adolescents—is sending explicit selfies. Homosexuality and transgenderism are the fullest outworkings of the selfie mindset—they are the completion of the erotic part of being "curved in on yourself." To offer a modern term, it is narcissexuality. Innate desire is the only truth. LGBTQ identities are judged especially good since they express innate desires. Here theological language is employed: Since God made ("oriented") me this way, it must be good. However, the Christian conception of the human person reveals man's desires as inherently (since the fall) distorted. To be "born this way" doesn't make it good. "No one does good, not even one" (Romans 3:12). The real ideological battle today centers around this issue.

Born for Eroticism

A primary reason our culture is at a crossroads is that while a portion of society still embraces a *mimetic* view of the world (see chapter 1) and recognizes that man's desires are disordered (as outlined in the previous chapter), a large part of the culture now believes the opposite:

man is by nature good, but the structures of society corrupt him. The cure for society, according to this way of thinking, is to allow people to embrace their first impulses. Instead of evaluating personal desires against the standard of natural law or revelation (e.g., the Decalogue), we should encourage people to follow their first impulses, wherever they lead. Only then will life be authentic. Man can be free only if there are no external influences on his decisions. Social, religious, and moral expectations are not options to be considered; they are enemies of freedom.

In past societies, particularly those of a generally Christian character, governing sexual relationships with social expectations and the force of law was considered imperative. The purpose of sexual ethics and laws was to preserve the institution of the family, protect women and children, and kept the peace. If the sexual revolution is to "liberate" people from these constraints, it is not enough to change or repeal laws and moral expectations surrounding sex. The foundations must be destroyed. The goal of the sexual revolution is not met merely by the acceptance of homosexuality or transgenderism. The goal is the destruction of the Christian religion.

It's tempting, but ultimately false, to tie the reformer Martin Luther to the philosophical thought leading us to where we are now on the brink of societal collapse. Certainly, some have used the great reformer for nefarious ends (or simply failed to grasp his aims). In this regard, Luther's famous speech at the 1521 Diet of Worms is frequently misunderstood. Luther was summoned before Emperor Charles V of the Holy Roman Empire to give an account for his writings, which called for reform. When Johann Eck demanded he recant, Luther declined, despite knowing it would likely lead to his execution. Here he uttered some of his most famous words,

"I cannot do otherwise, here I stand, may God help me, Amen."[46] The general myth surrounding these words is that Luther appealed to conscience. The later idea that personal conscience is the only arbiter of truth developed from this famous quote.

However, it is wrong to think Luther is the source of such an idea. Luther did indeed appeal to conscience, but it was a conscience fully informed by Holy Scripture:

> Unless I am convinced by the testimony of the Scriptures or by clear reason (for I do not trust either in the pope or in councils alone, since it is well known that they have often erred and contradicted themselves), I am bound by the Scriptures I have quoted and my conscience is captive to the Word of God. I cannot and I will not retract anything, since it is neither safe nor right to go against conscience.[47]

Conscience is a safe guide only when it is captive to the Word of God. As we saw in the previous chapter, man is born with disordered desires. While the Law of God is written on every man's heart, the decline of each human being, as sin grows within him, leads to self-justification for every misdeed. Man's conscience is unreliable unless it is formed and continually reformed by the Holy Spirit working through the Word.

What began to happen as the Western mind detached itself from Christian thought is a redefinition of conscience as natural instinct (or desire). Whereas the conscience formed by God's Word would condemn sexual activity outside of marriage, a conscience that is formed by natural instinct says the opposite: not

---

46 Martin Luther, *Luther's Works*, American Edition, vol. 32, *Career of the Reformer 2*, ed. George W. Forell and Helmut T. Lehmann (Philadelphia: Fortress Press, 1958), 113. The precise words that Luther said are disputed.

47 *Luther's Works*, vol. 32, 112.

only is sexual activity outside of marriage not a sin but it is also a positive good.

As Luther and others called for reform, some took this opportunity to rebel against Christianity itself. Over the next few centuries, the writings of the Old and New Testaments went from being regarded as the Word of God to words inhibiting natural desires. Poetry and literature took aim at marriage as an oppressive institution that prohibited people from finding genuine happiness. Examples of this are found in the poetry of William Wordsworth and Percy Shelley, and the novels of Thomas Hardy, particularly *Jude the Obscure*. Whereas the repression of acting on sexual desires prevented happiness, the work of Freud expanded the idea. To Freud, sex is not merely an activity, the fulfillment of one desire among others. Sex is identity. In the development of the human person, beginning with breastfeeding and defecation and moving on to masturbation and maturation (what Freud calls seeking genital pleasure), everything is sexual. To be human is to seek sexual pleasure. This is the Freudian *telos* for humanity: humans are born to fulfill their sexual desires. Happiness is eroticism.

Yet, for humanity to be free, according to this view, it is not enough to be able to seek this erotic "happiness." Any institution or truth-claim presenting a different understanding of happiness must be eradicated. We saw in the previous chapter that happiness as a modern value includes being free from suffering and any constraint of duty. The latest iterations of the sexual revolution—homosexual "marriage" and transgenderism—are not therefore about broadening the culture's understanding of acceptable sexual choices. Proponents of this view claim that marriage as a heterosexual monogamous institution must be destroyed for humans to be liberated. They also claim that marriage between a man and a woman is inherently repressive of the woman. To them, even a proper Christian understanding of marriage is unacceptable. This is because marriage as classically understood places demands on individuals—both husband and wife—to serve the greater good of the family. In traditional marriage vows, both man and wife pledge to live sacrificially toward the other in times of sickness, poverty, and any circumstance that is not better but "worse."

To the sexual revolutionaries, such vows are prisons that result in unhappy persons. In a *poietic* world, where the individual creates his own happiness, marriage is seen as repressive and an enemy to freedom. In such a world, social mores concerning sex, therefore, must be opposed and erased from human memory. For this reason, Christian bakers must be compelled to bake wedding cakes for "marriages" prohibited by Scripture and natural law, and florists likewise must be compelled to prepare arrangements. This worldview is not a matter of "live and let live," because the discussion really is not about practice or behavior. It is about identity. For the sexual revolutionaries, one cannot hate the sin but love the sinner; they are inextricably bound together, and to call it sin is the highest moral offense. Allowing contrary values to be expressed is heresy to the high priests of the sexual revolution and can serve only oppressive ends. Since man is understood to be primarily a psychological being, words and actions that reject how a person self-identifies are said to cause psychological harm. Any words that do not affirm a person's desires are viewed as violence. Those who commit such acts of "violence" must be canceled, reeducated, and even charged with crimes.

In this light, it is easy to see how traditional Christianity is not merely rejected as outmoded but is also considered harmful. The Scripture does "violence" to the human pursuing the happiness of eroticism because its commandments reject our selfish desires and instead point us to a different purpose of the human body.

Moving bodily through the earth, Christians see the world as infused with divine meaning. One's imagination is not for the self-creation of a unique individual. Instead, life's shape will look to the created pattern and enscripturated revelation for a model. Put simply, we shouldn't act on how we feel but on what God's Word tells us is true. To determine how life should be lived, we can look to the Ten Commandments. However, that is not all, as though life were simply a matter of following the rules. The Law exists to show us the good and give us a vision of our end.[48] Man was made to live in communion with God (Commandments 1–3, the "First Table" of the Law) and in self-giving love toward his neighbor (Commandments 4–10, the "Second Table" of the Law). Actions can be judged, and ethical decisions made, by seeing how they serve these ends. An individual can assess his life and see the distinction between who he is now and what he is intended to be.

The End of Marriage

This is true also of larger cultural institutions (some of which, such as marriage, we would see as divinely instituted). If marriage is only about companionship or sexual pleasure, then there is no reason to limit it to one member of each sex—or indeed, to two people at all. Three, or three hundred, humans could do just as well, pragmatism alone providing any limit. Since some people derive companionship (or even carnal pleasure, sometimes called *bestiality*[49]) from animals, why should marriage be limited to humans?

---

48 In this book, "end" in this context means not the moment when something is finished, but a goal, when something is brought to perfection or does fully that for which it was intended. The New Testament term for this is *telos*.

49 God's Word forbids sexual relationships between humans and animals; see, e.g., Leviticus 18:23; 20:15–16; Deuteronomy 27:21.

The enemies of our Creator seek the end, the destruction, of marriage. For this reason, it is necessary to reemphasize in our day the true end (the purpose, or *telos*) of marriage.

The *telos* of marriage includes procreation, not merely personal pleasure. This means there is every reason to limit it to the man and woman who can be father and mother. (We are not here speaking of that sad condition where a man and woman are not blessed by God with children, through no choice of their own.) Marriage's end is in reflecting the image of God in the one-flesh union, which results in the calling to parent the children born from the union.

Homosexual marriage, therefore, has a fundamentally different *telos*, and where *that* end is generally accepted by society, it will necessarily affect all marriages. Homosexual marriage would have been unthinkable in a society that did not embrace first the pleasure principle, which resulted in the acceptance of divorce, and then smaller families, where the pleasure of sex was decoupled from the natural outcome (i.e., children), and finally two people who express no desire for children.

That this other *telos* is already at work we can see in the widespread acceptance of divorce, even in the church. As a pastor, I've experienced many times the challenge of giving counsel to one or both spouses in a troubled marriage. In some cases, I've had the joy of seeing the acceptance of God's Word heal the marriage. In others, however, feelings are the ultimate moral arbiter. "It no longer feels right" is so culturally powerful that pastors and therapists are looked to simply to justify that feeling. Where that justification is not given—and especially where it is contradicted—then the pastor, church, or therapist is condemned for the cardinal sin of failing to validate the person's emotions.

Among the general populace, and even many Christians, the emotional decision is celebrated as courageous, and the things once prohibited are celebrated.

Pornography

If divorce and extra-marital sex reflect man being curved in on the self, pornography does so even more. It is a fantasy world where God's Word is specifically rejected. Pornography does more than simply encourage lust. It disconnects sex entirely from any relationship (however temporary). There is no meaning to it beyond the act itself. It is thus a repudiation of society itself, which has its foundation in the family—marriage resulting in child-rearing and the cross-generational society derived from it.

Abortion

The popularization of Freud's ideas moved sex from activity to identity. Through technological advancements in contraception and abortion—and with the legalization of the same—sex also became detached from its chief consequence, children. Yet the way I just framed that assumes the worldview of the sexual revolutionaries, who seek to free sex from any consequences. Referring to children as a consequence instead of a gift separates sex from procreation at its source. It assumes sex is first about pleasure. Dystopian novels like Aldous Huxley's *Brave New World* depict a world where this has come to fruition and children are generated in laboratories.

Where pornography destroys the end of marriage passively through complete disconnection from the family, abortion does so actively. The mindset of abortion is that children are disposable and unwanted. Birth control resists or avoids the natural fruit of holy marriage, but abortion murders the child God gave as a blessing.

Abortion is often presented as liberating women by freeing them from the "burden" of children so they can work without interruption alongside men. Yet abortion allows men to pursue sexual pleasure with no commitment to the woman. Abortion enables men to use and abuse women without emotional or financial investment.

Homosexuality

People who view sex as mere impulses to be acted on with whomever one wants to will often label objection to homosexuality as *homophobia*. This removes the issue from moral discourse because phobias are seen as irrational fears, not moral issues. Then, once they have severed sex from a meaningful act within a larger human *telos,* they see sexual expression as a matter of taste, outside the realm of objective goods or evils. To them, objections to homosexual (or any other kind of sexual) behavior denote irrational prejudices, not reasoned moral thinking. They see the person with the "phobia" as mentally ill and in need of therapy.

"Love is love" was one of the most effective slogans leading to the 2015 Obergefell v. Hodges ruling, whereby the Supreme Court of the United States invented a right to same-sex marriage. After the ruling, "Love Wins" was displayed on progressive church signs in my neighborhood. This notion of love is not unique to homosexual activism, but it has become ubiquitous anywhere love is equated with desire. The contemporary understanding of love is hardly distinguishable from selfishness. The object of this sort of love is essentially the means for personal indulgence. Our culture's definition of love is a twisted form of self-adoration. What I love exists to satisfy me. Love of pizza, whiskey, or sex becomes little different from loving a person.

When the pizza, or the person, no longer gives me pleasure, it is time to move on.

This is also certainly true of heterosexual relationships when the other person is objectified. A kind of contract is entered into whereby we make certain sacrifices to maintain the relationship. This, too, is selfish, and not unlike the bill we pay for mobile phone or internet service. We would prefer to keep the money but will certainly spend it as long as the pleasure data keeps streaming in. So, too, we will pay the cost of the upkeep of the relationship, as long as the pleasure we receive stays current with the cost we are paying.

I made a pastoral visit on a young woman who was about to leave her husband. He had recently begun suffering from a neurological problem and was no longer able to work. "I didn't sign up for this," she told me, thinking that as a reason to justify leaving her husband. But she did "sign up" for it. That's what the marriage vows mean (and why we shouldn't write our own). But the culture had already rewritten them long before, from "So long as we both shall live" to "So long as we both shall love." This sort of love has an exit clause; the pledge thereof is declared null and void when the pain starts exceeding the pleasure.

Homosexuality takes this notion of love one step further. This is in no way a personal indictment of those who experience homosexual desires, for all have sinned and fall short of the glory of God. Yet God's plan for holy marriage is—however miserably people fail in this regard—to be oriented away from the self toward the other. That's what *hetero* means: "other." *Homo*, by contrast, means "same." The person drawn to the same sex is drawn to a mirror image of the self. As introduced in the previous chapter, it is intrinsically narcissistic (although narcissism afflicts those of every sexual proclivity, to be sure).

Homosexual people have particular sexual inclinations. These inclinations do not negate the inherent dignity of the person but are a particular kind of defect. All humans since the fall of our first parents are defective. The sexual ethic of the Scriptures is intended still, even after the fall, to call us away from our defects toward genuine love, which is to be understood as self-sacrifice.

Only when we understand that the love that is in God, and that we are called to, is fulfilled in placing the needs of others ahead of ourselves, can we enter into any relationship rightly. Who you love is not about who you desire for the satisfaction of your lust, but who you faithfully serve within the boundaries of the Ten Commandments. Love can never be defined by one body part being placed into another. The One who is love shows us how to love in the Decalogue. Outside of that is only lust and self-adoration, regardless of what word we use to justify it.

A not-uncommon argument is that people are born with certain desires, and since they are born that way, they are justified in acting upon those desires. Currently, none of this has been demonstrated scientifically. But if a "gay gene" were found (for which some biologists have been searching), or if other particular sexual proclivities could be identified as having an origin from birth within a person, it would not negate a single word of the Scripture's teaching about human sexuality. This is only true, of course, if one recognizes the post-fall theological anthropology. As we saw in earlier chapters, humans are afflicted from conception with concupiscence (corrupt desires). That one person is inclined toward greed or anger or pride or lust or a myriad of sins is no surprise. The inclination is no justification for sin—any sin. Every human is called to repentance. The Lord's forgiveness is not dependent upon having only socially acceptable sinful inclinations. It is dependent entirely on the justifying death of the Lord Jesus. Those who, in contrition and repentance, believe and are baptized are called to reject their sinful inclinations, be they heterosexual or homosexual.

This is a hard message because the preaching of repentance is always difficult. The truth about ourselves hurts—whoever we are. The message that homosexual desire is a sin is regarded as profoundly hateful and backward in our culture. But genuine love requires us to be truthful.

That love requires us to be truthful about ourselves. For a very long time, Christians in America have tolerated many heterosexual sins, including sex outside of marriage, living together outside of marriage, and divorce. There is no cultural acceptance of homosexual marriage without a preceding cultural acceptance of divorce. Even within churches that have the correct doctrine on paper, a member who divorces a spouse without any scriptural justification can, if the pastor says it is a sin, find a home in a nearby church without any questions asked. In the American environment, where above all pastors are expected to be "nice" and congregations are in competition with one another for members, serious church discipline is nearly impossible.

Being truthful about ourselves also means telling those who struggle with homosexual desire that they are welcomed by the same Jesus who absolves those struggling against their heterosexual inclinations outside of marriage. Only when sinners with heterosexual sins include themselves fully within those who confess they are "sinful and unclean" unequivocally, as "chief of sinners," can those struggling against homosexual sin be sincerely welcomed into the company of redeemed sinners that is the Church our Lord Jesus established.

Conclusion

Eroticism does not fulfill its promise of happiness. The sexual relationship is a gift of God but can be utilized without sin only within the purpose for which it was created: holy marriage between one man and one woman open to procreation. Fornication, along with the LGBTQ rebellion against creation, is no victimless crime. It is an assault against the purpose of humanity. Nowhere is this more apparent than with transgenderism, the subject of our next chapter.

REFLECTION QUESTIONS

1. How does the belief that people are good but society is bad affect life in your church and community?

2. How did Luther understand *conscience* at the Diet of Worms? Is it the same way people speak of conscience today?

3. Can traditional marriage survive in a society that accepts other forms of so-called marriage?

4. How has violence been redefined?

5. What measure should we use to judge the actions of ourselves and others?

6. What is the *telos* of marriage?

7. How is the term *love* weaponized in contemporary debate?

8. What does *love* mean from a Christian perspective?

9. How can we respond to people who say, "I was born this way"?

10. How have churches treated some sexual sins as less sinful than others?

CHAPTER 6

RESPONDING TO THE TRANSGENDER REVOLUTION

Introduction

"A theologian of glory calls evil good and good evil. A theologian of the cross calls the thing what it actually is."[50] Never in the history of the world have we more needed brave people to call things what they actually are. A social contagion has spread through the West, causing children to mutilate their bodies and receive hormone treatments with drastic consequences. How did this happen? How can Christians respond? Are you willing to call a thing what it actually is, irrespective of the consequences?

Dude Looks like a Lady

Throughout history, people who identified—at least some of the time—as the opposite sex were not unknown. The term in use since 1911, *transvestite*, related particularly to clothing (as in the words *vest* and *vestment*). Popular music recognized this part of the community with songs like Aerosmith's 1987 hit "Dude (Looks like a Lady)." "Lola," the 1970 song by the English band the Kinks, caused no little controversy in describing a sexual encounter between a man and a trans woman. Today, any controversy would come from offering moral criticism of such a thing.

---

50 Martin Luther, "Heidelberg Disputation, 1518," *Luther's Works*, American Edition, vol. 31, *Career of the Reformer 1*, ed. Harold J. Grimm and Helmut T. Lehmann (Philadelphia: Fortress Press, 1957), 40.

Given that the time between 1970 to today is short within the span of human history, it may seem like the transgender revolution has been a rapid radical shift. Recognizing that the path to this point began long ago with existentialism (see chapter 1) involves understanding that the current transgender moment is the capstone of a centuries-long project. The aim of this has been to overthrow not only Christianity but also the idea of an objective human nature, natural law, and a purpose to human sexuality outside personal desire.

The transgender movement is such a capstone because it involves the final overthrow of biological reality. It claims that you are not what your chromosomes or sexual organs say you are. You are whatever you feel you are. You are what you create yourself to be. Your inner voice is the only truth. Freedom consists in the demand that others recognize your inner voice as your truth, regardless of what science says. Recall the passage we considered in chapter 1, Psalm 100:3: "It is He who made us, and not we ourselves." Transgenderism is the most overt renunciation of that confession. The fundamental change (*trans*) is not toward a specific sex or identity, but it is a change away from the Creator's intention. It is the triumph of a will not merely ignorant of God but also hostile to His creation. The will to change the body is the desire to destroy what God made and to build the opposite in its place.

To make such a move, a linguistic alteration needed to be introduced to shape popular thought. I mentioned that the common term in the twentieth century was *transvestite*. As sex-change operations became more prevalent, academia invented a radical separation between *sex* and *gender*. This separation attempted to distinguish between a person's physiology, particularly in the primary sexual characteristics, with that person's interior identity (gender). By the opening decade of the twenty-first century, hordes of students had been indoctrinated with the mantra "Gender is a social construct."

Changes in language are natural and are always occurring. However, the particular kind of linguistic changes in our era are unnatural in two ways: they are being forced upon us by edicts from "elites" and they deny basic reality. Newspeak is here, only a few decades behind schedule.[51] For example, it is natural to refer to females about to give birth as "pregnant women." In an era seeking to disconnect itself from nature (and nature's God), such a term cannot be used, since it implies (rightly) that males cannot give birth. When madness prevails, however, then a term such as "birthing people" is imposed. Similar awkward constructions such as "people with uteruses" likewise demand entry into today's stilted lexicon.

Leftist theologians had long been doing this by reframing how they spoke (and taught others to speak) about God. Consider the well-known passage, "For God so loved the world, that He gave His only Son, that whoever believes in Him should not perish but have eternal life" (John 3:16). The problematic masculine pronouns must go, so the theologians of the revolution rework passages: "For God so loved the world, that God gave God's only child, that whoever believes should not perish but have authentic life." Denuding the gendered language was an important step in changing how people viewed God and themselves.[52]

The separation of gender from sex generates confusion in those whose personalities do not land in the middle of cultural expectations for male or female behaviors and interests. Not long ago, a

---

51 In George Orwell's *Nineteen Eighty-Four*, Newspeak was invented as an altered form of English to control thought in Oceania.

52 See William Oddie, *What Will Happen to God? Feminism and the Reconstruction of Christian Belief* (San Francisco: Ignatius Press, 1988).

girl who liked sports and eschewed playing with dolls was typically called a "tomboy." Feminine expression was understood to have a spectrum, and there was no confusion that a girl who roughhouses with boys might just be a boy. Similarly, the bookish boy who shied away from sports might be derided as a "nerd," but he wasn't confused with a girl. The boy who can't hit a baseball and the boy who can't read a book were both *boys*, determined not by their individual personalities or gifts but by their biological characteristics. Today, such children outside of the mainstream may be told from early childhood that they might be trapped "in the wrong body."[53]

In a society that prizes uniqueness and inner experience above all else, with cultural pressure applied by everyone from public school teachers to airlines and candy companies, it is hardly surprising that many children adopt the latest craze sweeping their generation. With the age of childhood now extended to 25 by government insurance regulations and car-rental companies, time spent on the quest for one's true identity is extended. In previous generations, many men and women by age 25 already had careers; many men had achieved the status of war veteran, husband, and father, and many women that of wife and mother. When meaning is defined by feelings, childhood is extended indefinitely, and everything is sexualized, confusion over identity is inevitable.

This problem is exacerbated by human existence being reduced to gender and sexuality by the sexual revolutionaries. Since this is a matter of will and not body, the transgender revolution is the final triumph of the Gnostic conception of reality, which subordinates the body to the soul and renders the material world something from which we must be liberated. Once one accepts the premise that a biological male can be a woman born into the wrong (i.e.,

---

53   See Abigail Shrier, *Irreversible Damage: The Transgender Craze Seducing Our Daughters* (Washington, DC: Regnery, 2020).

male) body, then it follows that the body is a prison. A person's true identity is entirely disconnected from creation.[54]

That feeling of being in the "wrong" body is called *gender dysphoria*. People who identify as transgender seek recognition of the dysphoria. This recognition is felt to be required to validate their identity. Transgender people perceive the rejection of how they identify as a rejection of their personhood. They feel invalidated and like violence has been committed against them. As they do with every human affliction, disciples of Jesus must be compassionate with those who experience this dysphoria. At the same time, it is necessary to call it what it is: an illness of the mind. Those who suffer from other mental illnesses, such as depression or social anxiety, are affirmed as human beings loved by God who happen to have minds that are disordered. We affirm the person but not the disorder. It would be the height of cruelty to affirm the disorder. Until recently, this was obvious. For mental health professionals, however, it is now dangerous and possibly career-ending to affirm such a thing. Laws are beginning to target pastoral counseling as well, forbidding the teaching of the biblical vision for humankind to those afflicted with homosexual desires or gender dysphoria. Misgendering someone is "thoughtcrime." We have always been at war with Eastasia.[55]

Nevertheless, "We must obey God rather than men" (Acts 5:29). And we must present the positive vision of God's *telos* for man. While expertise in counseling is extremely important, as

---

54   An extremely small percentage of people are born in an intersex condition, where sexual organs are ambiguous and/or chromosomal patterns do not match one of the male/female binary. These disorders require compassion, in the same way we show compassion for those with other disabilities or abnormalities. The existence of intersex people does not negate the pattern of creation where God made humanity male and female.

55   In Orwell's *Nineteen Eighty-Four*, using the "wrong" language was thoughtcrime, as was denying basic reality when the state demanded that one articulate something different. When the country changes its enemy from Eurasia to Eastasia, it insists all citizens affirm, "We have always been at war with Eastasia." Affirming what is false is the ultimate submission to the authority of the elites.

is speaking compassionately, it is incumbent on all Christians to speak the truth and point people toward the healing power of the sacraments and the promise of resurrection, when all things are made new (see Revelation 21:5).

Why Are So Many People Identifying as Trans?

The reasons are many, but here are some of the most common:

Discomfort with One's Body

Teenagers who feel bad about their bodies are told this is a sign they are trans. For example, some teen girls who have eating disorders hear—often through social media or websites designed for grooming teens—that the true source of their discomfort is that they are not recognizing that they are trans. Even discomfort with the sound of one's voice may be identified as a sign of gender dysphoria. Anyone who has gone through puberty, and the social awkwardness around peers during this time, knows what it is to be uncomfortable in a changing body. The sexual revolutionaries know this and take advantage of this time to indoctrinate children in the LGBTQ worldview.

"Cis" Is Evil

Cisgender is a novel term invented in the late twentieth century through "gender studies." Created to describe people who identify with the "gender" that at birth was "assigned" to them, the term has come to be synonymous with a privileged oppressor. Some surveys now show public school teenagers nearly universally identifying themselves as LGBTQ because of the cultural stigma attached to being "cis."

Self-Expression

Gender has been redefined by the cultural revolutionaries. The new orthodoxy demands not thinking in binary categories in either sex or gender. They make a further distinction between gender identity and gender expression. Gender identity is understood as a personal sense of self, one's own self-conception. Gender expression is how one presents oneself to the world. This can change from day to day, or even throughout the day. A myriad of genders are available to create a seemingly unique expression of self: gender fluid (reflecting both genders at the same time or in turn; demigirl (mostly girl, but some boy); demiboy (mostly boy, but some girl); transmale/transboy (a female identifying as a male); transfemale/transgirl (a male identifying as a female); agender (a person who rejects the idea of having a gender); aliagender (a person who claims no existing gender but something beyond current definitions); bigender (a person who identifies as two different genders); two-spirit (an American Indian designation for two genders residing in the same person); graygender (a person who experiences ambivalence about gender); intergender (a person who identifies as falling between different gender categories); multi-gender (experiencing multiple gender identities); pangender/omnigender (experiencing many or all gender identities); and numerous others. A review of gender listings on various medical websites and social media identifiers reveals an ever-expanding listing of genders in the last decade, with lists ranging from seven up to seventy-two, which will no doubt be out of date by the time this is printed.

Opposition to Parental Rights

Since man's fall into sin, children have rebelled against their parents. This is nothing new. The Fourth Commandment had application long before it was chiseled into stone. What has changed is the encroaching role of the state. The sexual revolutionaries, blending Marxism with Freudianism, know that to change society they must separate children from the mores of their parents. Public schools are hotbeds of LGBTQ activism, often directly opposing the wishes of parents. A recent political campaign in my home state of Virginia featured one candidate who insisted that parents should not be allowed to tell schools what they should teach. As the sexual revolutionaries seek to drive a wedge between parental rights and the authority of government, the emotional and sexual turmoil of adolescence is fertile ground for fomenting rebellion against parents by encouraging students to identify as LGBTQ.

Irrevocable Desecration

"Do you not know that your body is a temple of the Holy Spirit within you, whom you have from God? You are not your own, for you were bought with a price. So glorify God in your body" (1 Corinthians 6:19–20). Man was made in the image of God. His body is thus intended for holiness. Every human body is to be honored and valued. The body of the baptized Christian, especially, is sacred.

What happens in transgender surgery is therefore nothing short of desecration. Phalloplasty or vaginoplasty destroys that part of the body God made for participation in His work of procreation. The voluntary mutilation of a woman's body through "top surgery" (mastectomy) transgender surgery removes from the young woman the possibility of breastfeeding future children. These decisions made by teenagers are permanent and irrevocable. The children making such decisions are not neurologically developed enough to be certain they will not feel differently within a few years. Often, these same children are too young to vote, drink alcohol, or purchase a firearm. Allowing them to make life-altering decisions to mutilate their own bodies is unconscionable.

What then makes it possible for medical professionals, mental health professionals, and educators to allow children to make such decisions? To abandon the obvious biological distinction between male and female, there is a prior philosophical move that needs to take place, namely, the rejection of the concept of objective truth. Prevalent in our society is the loss of the definite article in front of *truth*, and a persistent modification. Gone is *the* truth, replaced with *my* truth, *your* truth, *their* truth. Fluid and malleable, truth is changed as often as underwear, and with greater stench.

It is imperative to remember that we have access to two kinds of truth: natural truth and revealed truth. The scientific method of observation and deduction shows us such things as the law of gravity, the three states of matter (solid, liquid, and gas), and that there are two sexes of humans (male and female), with distinguishing characteristics of each. These truths in nature show us *what* is real in our world. Revealed truth, given to us by God through inspiration and recorded in the Holy Scriptures, shows us *why* things are as they are, as well as the truth about the spiritual realm. One need not be a Christian to discern that objects in motion stay in motion (Newton's first law of physics), but the Christian Scriptures show us God's meaning for the world, and specifically for man's purpose in it.

Recalling that Jesus is "the way, and the truth, and the life" (John 14:6), and that the Father's Word is truth (John 17:17), we will respond differently when variously confronted with lies about God, man, and the world. Consider the response of Jesus to Pontius Pilate's query, "What is truth?" (John 18:38). Jesus remained silent.

The same was true in the face of false accusations. "He gave him no answer, not even to a single charge" (Matthew 27:14). When in a conversation with someone who appears open to hearing you, then the apostolic admonition applies, to speak the truth in love (Ephesians 4:15).

It will likely profit no one to spend time in internet jousting with activists for the sexual revolution. Questions on both sides of internet debates are likely insincere, and most conversations generate more heat than light. There are many reasons to not participate in social media, and conflict with ideologues is one of them. Some people only want to see the world burn. The unproductive arguments that take place on the internet often poison the soul and edify no one. How then can you dialogue with a person on the other side of these debates? First, remember your own sins. In your daily prayers, confess and cry out for help regarding the temptations that have held mastery over you. Second, remember that a person captivated by LGBTQ ideology is someone for whom Christ died, someone who struggles with questions of identity, meaning, and self-worth. Third, approach a person in a spirit of genuine care and humility. In her book *The Secret Thoughts of an Unlikely Convert*,[56] Rosaria Butterfield chronicles how her journey out of lesbianism toward Christianity began with a kind letter from a local pastor, later followed by a dinner invitation from the pastor and his wife. Thus began a long friendship, with deep conversations about literature, hermeneutics, hospitality, and ultimately theology. Butterfield's conversion did not happen in an instant but through countless conversations matched with genuine friendship. This leads to the fourth principle of such dialogues: patience. Changes in worldview cannot happen in a hurry. Worldviews are

---

56 Rosaria Champagne Butterfield, *The Secret Thoughts of an Unlikely Convert: An English Professor's Journey into Christian Faith* (Pittsburg: Crown and Covenant, 2012).

formed over time, and it takes time for trust to develop before presuppositions can be questioned.

Conclusion

Always with love, God calls Christians to call things what they really are. Men are men, women are women, and these are immutable truths. Jesus is the truth (John 14:6). If what He says is not true, then nothing is. The Nicene Creed confesses about Him, *et homo factus est*: "And He was made man." The incarnation of the Son of God is for the healing of the human race. He heals every dysphoria, and His redemption is for every tribe, tongue, people, and nation. The divisions of those tribes and tongues, and how they are reconciled in Christ, is the next subject of our study.

REFLECTION QUESTIONS

1. What does transgenderism say about the doctrine of creation?

2. Why is it important to be truthful in the language we use?

3. Why are people suddenly identifying as trans at such high rates?

4. What are the various ways *truth* is used? Why is it important to be careful about this?

5. How should we approach conversations with people who disagree with us?

RACE AND CULTURE

Introduction

The discussion of race is everywhere today. Critical Race Theory, steeped in Marxism, is stoking the fires of resentment and dividing people anew by skin color. Since all human beings come from a single union—the marriage of Adam and Eve—all humans have the same dignity and worth. It is ultimately unhelpful to speak about different groupings of people as "races." This suggests a similar distinction between humans as there is between different species of animals or birds. Saying that people are of different origins and are radically *other* leads to dehumanizing those people. This technique effectively prepares for conflict with and violence against the *other*. Christianity recognizes that while there are different people groups descended from various families and divided especially by language, there is truly one human family descended from Adam. By His incarnation, Christ assumes into His person the human nature. He is the new Adam in whom, for the entire human race, is redemption—and ultimate reunion.

Critical Race Theory

Critical Race Theory (CRT) is an outgrowth of postmodernism from the twentieth century, which in turn emerged from the Critical Theory political ideology of the 1920s and '30s. In the original demonic appeal in the Garden of Eden, our first parents were deceived into resenting

God as the hierarch. They believed He was withholding good from them. Critical Theory is infected with a similar demonic appeal, stoking resentment against others. Its goal is to root out the hidden ways that society oppresses those lower in the hierarchy. In this way of seeing the world, oppression is built into every fabric of the societal system, hence Critical Theory's talk about "systemic" oppression.

CRT asserts that the problem is not in overt racial prejudice but in a racialized system of oppression ("systemic racism") that governs all of society while remaining hidden even from the oppressors. Identifying and dismantling these systems of oppression is the goal of those fighting against this injustice. Such racialized warriors are part of a larger movement termed "Social Justice." Radical adherents to CRT dedicate all interactions to eradicating "whiteness"/systemic racism, homophobia, transphobia, and other sorts of things they label as oppressive. With religious zeal, they are overtly hostile to traditional Christianity, while at the same time they are found within church bodies like the Evangelical Lutheran Church in America, Presbyterian Church (USA), the Episcopal Church, and the United Methodist Church (which, as of this writing, is in the process of separating into three separate denominations).

It is true that the use of racial categories was historically used as justification for the enslavement of Africans, along with the development of the colonial system by European powers. While enslavement and land conquests have happened throughout history, in most cases the specific makeup of people's skin color and other ethnic physical characteristics were seen as secondary environmental characteristics, not inherent racial differences. Atrocities were conducted on the basis of perennial sins like greed. European colonialism in the latter half of the second millennium, however, began to emphasize biological characteristics as inherited, not environmental, paving the way for the belief that certain people groups are inherently inferior. This gave rise to modern ideas of race and racism. Such views are absolutely evil and have no place in the mind of any Christian. The Scriptures clearly teach that every human being has worth and dignity and that we are all part of a common human family stemming from the first parents, who are the ancestors of every human being.

Racism nevertheless continues to be a dominant motif in today's cultural conflicts. Christians have much to contribute here as in the past. Abolitionist movements on both sides of the Atlantic were driven by Christians such as William Wilberforce (1759–1833), who rejected the colonialist notions of inherited racial inferiority. It took a century after the American Civil War (1861–65) for America to fully address the continuing racism in its population, culminating in the Civil Rights Act of 1964. By the 1970s, however, academics were making significant strides in turning their students against classical liberalism. Academics from the "Frankfurt School" fled Nazi Germany in the late 1930s, finding a home in American universities, particularly Columbia University in New York City.[57] Turning Critical Theory toward race, CRT rejected Martin Luther King Jr.'s vision of a colorblind society. CRT questions every aspect of the economic and political history of the US government, including the Constitutional protections of freedom of speech and free exercise of religion.

Under CRT, equality is replaced with equity. Instead of equality of opportunity, and equal treatment under the law, equity demands

---

57   See Michael Walsh, *The Fiery Angel: Art, Culture, Sex, Politics, and the Struggle for the Soul of the West* (New York: Encounter Books, 2018), and Andy Ngo, *Unmasked: Inside Antifa's Radical Plan to Destroy Democracy* (New York: Center Street, 2021).

the same outcome for everyone. However, because of the historic mistreatment of minority groups, minorities must achieve more favorable outcomes than whites in order to remedy past injustices. CRT also rejects other aspects of America's founding, such as rationalism and a neutral application of the constitution.

Race, in the CRT worldview, is a social construct developed to protect white privilege and supremacy. All progress that has been made in race relations in America, argued Derrick Bell,[58] has been due to "interest convergence," where blacks received social advancements only because it was in the interest of whites.[59] Also included in this worldview is that embedded in the white subconscious is the urge to do everything in their power to maintain power. Further, even desegregation was regarded as fundamentally racist. As CRT developed in the late twentieth century, its activists began to demand safe spaces, decry microaggressions, and work against freedom of speech by inventing a category of hate speech.

CRT's outlook is that virtually all people of color experience every day the oppression of racism. It posits that the entire legal and social system of America is centered around preserving white supremacy. This is so embedded that it is hidden, requiring the services of experts to expose and dismantle the systems of racism. They believe that people of color (along with other categories of oppressed peoples) alone have the full competence to see and understand systemic oppression, and therefore their voices are required in every organization and conversation. Further, since people of color are inherently the oppressed, not the oppressors, then it is impossible for a person of color to be racist. In this view, only whites are racist. Objection to this is proof of "white" privilege

---

58 Bell is considered by many to be the father of CRT.
59 See Derrick Bell, *And We Are Not Saved: The Elusive Quest for Racial Justice* (New York: Basic Books, 1989).

and "white" oppression. Under these narrow terms, conversation is impossible. In a tragic irony, the ideology that gave rise to racism—that certain people groups are inherently inferior—is adopted with slight modification by CRT: the dominant demographic, "white" people as a group, is inherently and universally oppressive. This extreme ideology of CRT does not solve racism. It deepens the divide.

Indoctrination: Schools, Parenting, and Pedagogy

In the 1970s and '80s, I went to public schools from kindergarten through my first year of college. Experiences vary, but most people I talk with who had similar experiences during this time (and a decade or so afterward) have a generally positive experience. It wasn't a Christian environment by any means, but it was a decent education. There were leftist teachers, but there were also conservatives. Ideology did not dominate the curriculum.

Those with similar experiences tend to begin with a basic trust in the public education system. Parents assume their children will receive roughly the same education they did, albeit with the added complications of technology and social media. If that isn't enough reason to send your children to the public schools, finances usually seal the deal. Why should parents spend large sums of money on a private or Christian school when their children will receive a good education for free, in addition to access to all of the extracurricular programs such as sports, music, and drama? It's simply not affordable, the thinking goes.

That equation is wrongly formed. Today, generally speaking, Christian parents cannot afford to send their children to the "free" public school. The cost is that child's mind (and body). Most schools have become indoctrination centers devoted to the sexual revolution and the implementation of Marxist ideals. The vision of Freud has come to pass. In his book *The Future of an Illusion*, Freud saw two particular problems in the education of children: the failure to help children develop sexually and the inculcation of religion. Broadly speaking, public schools in America today have understood the assignment: children from the very earliest levels are taught to affirm all things LGBTQ (and question their own identity), while the Christian faith is banned from the conversation.

One evening, I was walking out of a classroom where I had just finished teaching a catechism class at church. We have a parochial school at my church, but these students attended public school. One student was aghast as I unconsciously tossed an empty aluminum can into a trash can. "Pastor! You didn't recycle!" I'm not against recycling, by any means. But what struck me here was the stridency with which the child condemned the sin against the commandment "Thou shalt recycle," while utterly failing to learn the assigned memory work from God's Ten Commandments. The lesson was clear in an instant: the real catechism lessons (through no personal fault, although the parents bear the responsibility) were taught in the public school, while what I was teaching was merely the means to attain the familial expectation of the Rite of Confirmation. The commandments to recycle, reduce the carbon footprint, embrace socialism, and accept the LGBTQ revolution had already been learned by heart, while God's commandments were optional. The child was quite nice, to be sure, but dropped out of church a few years after confirmation. The years of cultural catechesis took their toll: the parents divorced and the children drifted. I bet, however, they still recycle.

I write this not to condemn them per se. I bear much of the

responsibility. I should have rebuked the parents earlier but found it easier to simply go along. In the northern Virginia suburbs of Washington, DC, where the price of real estate is astronomical, the temptation is to buy a big house far out in the distant exurbs. This means a long drive (in some cases more than an hour) to get to church. Attending a Christian school is impractical. These parents trade a serious Christian upbringing for a comfortable, luxurious dwelling at a lower cost. It seems like a lifestyle choice, but only later, after seeing the effects, did I fully realize it is sin.

What was necessary several decades ago is critical now: live near your church and send your children to a Christian school or homeschool them. It may require sacrifice—significant financial and lifestyle sacrifice. You may need to live in a smaller home, take a more modest vacation, or cancel your streaming services with their monthly bills (you should probably cancel them anyway, as they likely fund degeneracy and are destroying your mind). Whatever sacrifice you are making is nothing compared to the loss of your children's faith. What shall it profit a man if he gains a large new home and forfeits his children's souls?

A father whose children abandoned Christianity in college once said, "I don't know what more I could have done. I took them to confirmation class." A one-hour class during seventh and eighth grades will never overcome the everyday stream of indoctrination during thirteen years of the K–12 environment. And then, like a successful big-league closer in the ninth inning, the "higher education" curriculum, steeped in cultural Marxism, takes the mound to seal the deal on total indoctrination.

Critical Race Theory (and other Critical Theories) advocates have focused much of their energy on the transformation of education in America. Issues like test-taking, discipline in classrooms, history and social curricula, and grading are all affected by CRT advocates within the educational systems, from kindergarten to graduate schools at once-elite universities. For example, the classicist Victor Davis Hanson documents how even some classics programs at top graduate schools have ceased traditional studies, focusing instead on subjects such as transgenderism in Homer's *Odyssey*.[60]

Many university programs, particularly in the field of pedagogy, focus on creating activist teachers. Thus, even at the kindergarten level in your local public school, it's very possible your child's teacher has an agenda outside of the formation of early reading and math skills: that of indoctrinating your child in queer theory, anti-Christian morality, and racial divisiveness under the cloak of anti-racism, generally with the support of the administration and school board. Children deserve to be in an environment that respects all people and emphasizes learning the foundational disciplines. Do everything you can to create this kind of environment in your local Christian school. Choosing a school is the most important parenting decision parents make. It is important to choose one that does not undo all your child learns in the Sunday or midweek teaching program of your church.

The Scriptural View of the Human Family

The first book of the Bible, Genesis, tracks family lines. As the human race grew, larger groupings of peoples derived from place names or tribal identifications, often from the name of a patriarch. Nevertheless, God's Word keeps ever before us the union of the human race in its beginning and its end, when the human race is reunited in one family, one Church. The new song of the heavenly

---

60 Victor Davis Hanson and John Heath, *Who Killed Homer: The Demise of Classical Education and the Recovery of Greek Wisdom* (New York: Encounter Books, 2001).

liturgy praises the Lamb, whose death effected this reunion: "Worthy are You to take the scroll and to open its seals, for You were slain, and by Your blood You ransomed people for God from *every tribe and language and people and nation*, and You have made them a kingdom and priests to our God, and they shall reign on the earth" (Revelation 5:9–10, emphasis added).

These nations became divided in the family of Noah, descending from his three sons, Shem, Ham, and Japheth (Genesis 10), then scattered following the confusion of languages at the tower of Babel (Genesis 11). Shem is the grandfather of Eber (from whom we get the name of his children, the *Hebrews*) and an ancestor of Abram, the patriarch of the Jews. Thus, the Jews descend from Shem. Ham is the father of Canaan, from whom come the Canaanites, later largely destroyed. This leaves Japheth, from whom come all other peoples, or "the nations."

After Ham's unspeakable wickedness toward his parents in uncovering his father's nakedness, Ham was condemned: "Cursed be Canaan; a servant of servants shall he be to his brothers" (Genesis 9:25). Ham's children, the Canaanites, increased in wickedness and refused to repent. These are the people who, in the time of Joshua and the judges, practiced ancestor worship, necromancy, ritual prostitution, and child sacrifice. The later destruction of the Canaanites in the conquest of Joshua, sometimes derided as barbaric, was the result of generations of hatred for God and His Word, continuing the first sexual perversion of Canaan's sin. This line of rebellion is foreseen in the curse on Canaan.

In the blessing of Noah's other two sons, however, is the prophecy of the ultimate union of the human race: "Blessed be the LORD, the God of Shem; and let Canaan be his servant. May God enlarge Japheth, and let him dwell in the tents of Shem, and let Canaan be his servant" (Genesis 9:26–27). In Shem are Abraham and the whole of the Jewish people, the Israelites. In Japheth, therefore, we have the figure of the Gentiles, the "nations" to whom the Lord Jesus sends His holy apostles: "All authority in heaven and on earth has been given to Me. Go therefore and make disciples of all nations, baptizing them in the name of the Father and of the Son and of the Holy Spirit, teaching them to observe all that I have commanded you" (Matthew 28:18–20).

Throughout the Old Testament, this ultimate reunion of the human race is prophesied. The prophet Isaiah especially extols the glory of God's grace to the Gentiles, foreseeing their reunion: "He will raise a signal for *the nations* [or *Gentiles*] and will assemble the banished of *Israel*" (Isaiah 11:12, emphasis added). This anticipates the Nunc Dimittis of Simeon: "Lord, now You are letting Your servant depart in peace, according to Your word; for my eyes have seen Your salvation that You have prepared in the presence of *all peoples*, a light for revelation to the *Gentiles*, and for glory to Your people *Israel*" (Luke 2:29–32, emphasis added). Isaiah 9:1–2 refers to a specific region, "Galilee of the nations" (ESV note: "Galilee of the Gentiles"), which is singled out for glory in the time when the Lord lifts the gloom from the world, the light that Simeon saw in the infant Jesus: "The people who walked in darkness have seen a great light; those who dwelt in a land of deep darkness, on them has light shone." In Jesus, the reunion of the nations is begun, and the Gentiles and Jews live as one family. Japheth returns home to dwell in the tents of Shem.

The company of the redeemed do not find their chief identity in their tribe, language, culture, or color. They are brothers and sisters because they are begotten anew from God: "To all who did receive Him [the Word, the Second Person of the Trinity], who believed in His name, He gave the right to become children of God, who were born, not of blood nor of the will of the flesh nor of the will of man, but of God" (John 1:12–13). Born of God, all those in this new family have a common Father, with the God-man Jesus as their elder brother.

The reunion of the world's families is triggered by the arrival of the nations ("the Greeks") to Jesus just before His crucifixion: "Now among those who went up to worship at the feast were some Greeks. So these came to Philip, who was from Bethsaida in Galilee, and asked him, 'Sir, we wish to see Jesus.' Philip went and told Andrew; Andrew and Philip went and told Jesus. And Jesus answered them, 'The hour has come for the Son of Man to be glorified'" (John 12:20–23). In John's Gospel, the glorification of Jesus is His death on the cross. There He reigns as King, having been crowned with the curse and announced to be "the man" (John 19:5). At the arrival of representatives of the nations, Jesus announces that His cross is the rallying point, the standard under which all the families of the earth will gather: "Now is the judgment of this world; now will the ruler of this world be cast out. And I, when I am lifted up from the earth, will draw all people to Myself" (John 12:31–32).

On the Day of Pentecost, the Holy Spirit was poured out on the apostles, and they spoke in other languages. The languages (or "tongues") were not unknown and mysterious. People "from every nation under heaven" (Acts 2:5) had gathered in Jerusalem for the festival. They heard the apostles preach "the mighty works of God" (v. 11) in their own languages. This reversal of the confusion of languages at the tower of Babel (Genesis 11) is another sign that in Jesus the human family is being gathered again into one. This theme continues in the preaching of the apostle Paul. In his sermon on Mars Hill in Athens, Paul emphasized that all human beings have a common father, Adam: "He [God] made from one man every nation of mankind to live on all the face of the earth" (Acts 17:26). An interesting variant[61] has the word "blood," stressing that all men are "blood brothers": "He [God] made from one *blood* every nation of mankind." Thus, it would be unthinkable for St. Paul to speak of the "white race" or the "black race" or any other. We were made from one man and share one blood. The Lord Jesus took on that human nature and shared in our flesh and blood. Both in Adam and again in Christ, the Scriptures everywhere teach the equal dignity of each human life regardless of incidental characteristics such as place of birth or eye, hair, or skin color.

In Adam, the human race sinned. In Adam, the human race was evicted from Eden. In Adam, the human race was denied access to the tree of life. In its sin, humanity was divided. Families became rivals. Nations became enemies. Their warring needs to be healed. By the blood of the Lamb, all humanity is invited to the healing tree and the cessation of the curse:

> Then the angel showed me the river of the water of life, bright as crystal, flowing from the throne of God and of the Lamb through the middle of the street of the city; also, on either side of the river, the tree of life with its twelve kinds of fruit, yielding its fruit each month. The leaves of the tree were for the healing of the nations. No longer will there be anything accursed, but the throne of God and of the Lamb will be in it, and His servants will worship Him. (Revelation 22:1–3)

What then shall we say about tensions among people groups

---

61 The manuscripts of the New Testament show remarkable agreement among the many copies that spread throughout the world in the first centuries after their writing. Occasional differences occur, which can further illumine (as in this case) the meaning. God made us from one man (Adam), and we all share one bloodline.

in modern Western nations, especially in the United States? It is imperative that we acknowledge the truth that America lived with the evil of slavery, which contradicted her ideals that all men are created equal. The maltreatment of those of African descent in slavery is a shameful part of her history. America's treatment of other groups at different times, including Chinese, Irish, Italian, and other immigrants, is also shameful. The First and Second World Wars fostered some horrible abuses of those of German and Japanese heritage. It seems almost comical now, but I recall my German relatives in Minnesota describing past ethnic tensions between Germans, Swedes, and Norwegians.[62]

We can take a lesson from one of the great theologians of the twentieth century, Hermann Sasse. A German who eventually emigrated to Australia, Sasse is regrettably lesser known than others who resisted the evils of National Socialism. But he did so at great cost, knowing how offensive it would be to "German morality." In the *Kirchenkampf* ("church struggle" in the 1930s), Lutheran pastors in Germany like Martin Niemöler and Dietrich Bonhoeffer are well-known for standing up to the National Socialists and their "German Christian" sympathizers. Though not as well-known, Hermann Sasse was (in this author's judgment) theologically superior. In 1932, his denunciation of the "Aryan Paragraph" (which excluded Jews from civil service and other public rights) was scathing:

> One can perhaps forgive National Socialism all its theological sins, but this article 24 [of the National Socialist party platform] excludes any possibility of a dialogue with the church, whether Protestant or

---

62 The 2005 film *Sweet Land* captures well the American immigrant experience in the Midwest as a German woman struggles to find acceptance in a Norwegian community.

Catholic.... [We teach regarding original sin that] the newborn infant of the noblest Germanic descent, endowed in body and mind with the optimal racial characteristics, is as much subject to eternal damnation as the genetically gravely compromised half-caste, from two decadent races. And we must go on to confess that the doctrine of the justification of the sinner *sola gratia, sola fide*, is the end of Germanic morality just as it is the end of all human morality.... We are not much interested in whether the Party gives its support to Christianity, but we would like to know whether the church is to be permitted to preach the Gospel in the Third Reich without let or hindrance, whether, that is, we will be able to continue undisturbed in our insults to the Germanic or Germanistic moral sense, as with God's help we intend to do.[63]

Sasse attacks the "Germanic morality" that would elevate one ethnic group above others. The preaching of man's universal sinfulness is an "insult" to the "Germanistic moral sense." It still is today. This is what the Law of God does: it insults us, that is, it shows us our sin and how much we need a Savior. *Lex semper accusat*: the Law always accuses.

Here then is how we should think about "race":

1. The doctrine of creation teaches us that we have one God and one common father and mother.

---

63 English text quoted from *The Third Reich and the Christian Churches*, ed. Peter Matheson (Grand Rapids, MI: Eerdmans, 1981), 2; also quoted in Hermann Sasse, *Letters to Lutheran Pastors*, vol. 1. (St. Louis: Concordia Publishing House, 2013), lxii.

2. The doctrine of original sin teaches us that we are all sinful. There is no difference; all have sinned and fall short of the glory of God.

3. The doctrine of Christ teaches us that God assumed the human nature into Himself. In the Nicene Creed, the Church confesses *et homo factus est* ("and was made man"). This includes every human person.

4. The doctrine of the Gospel teaches us that every tribe, tongue, and ethnicity is included, without distinction: "Go therefore and make disciples of all nations, baptizing them in the name of the Father and of the Son and of the Holy Spirit" (Matthew 28:19); "A light for revelation to the Gentiles, and for glory to Your people Israel" (Luke 2:32); "There is neither Jew nor Greek, there is neither slave nor free, there is no male and female, for you are all one in Christ Jesus" (Galatians 3:28).

The teachings of Christianity will be an "insult" to American morality, just as they were to the German morality. When you are found to believe such "insults," it may cost you your job, your reputation, and a boatload in legal fees. Fear not. "And take they our life, Goods, fame, child, and wife, Though these all be gone, Our vict'ry has been won; The Kingdom ours remaineth."[64]

Luther's Jewish Problem

The preceding section demonstrates well how twentieth-century Lutherans rejected anti-Semitism. It is no secret that Martin Luther, the great reformer, said inexcusable things about the Jews,

---

64 Martin Luther, "A Mighty Fortress Is Our God" (*LSB* 656:4).

most notably in his 1543 writing *On the Jews and Their Lies*. Already at the time of publication, prominent reformers Philip Melanchthon and Andreas Osiander were displeased with it.[65] Earlier in his career, Luther's 1523 treatise *That Jesus Christ Was Born a Jew* was well received by contemporary Jews.[66] Various excuses and justifications have been made for Luther on this topic. On the other side, Luther has been blamed for inspiring the Holocaust.[67] Only two things need to be said here. First, we must show honor and respect to all the sons and daughters of Abraham on account of their common humanity and especially because through them were given the Torah, the Psalms, and the prophecies of the Savior, and through the seed of Abraham and the line of their great king David came the Lord Jesus Christ in the flesh. Second, it is a great benefit that Lutherans have no infallible teacher as the papists do. No pastor, leader, or reformer is without sin. When they err, we are free to reject the error with no damage to the faith.

Conclusion

"In your offspring shall all the nations of the earth be blessed" (Genesis 22:18). This promise to Abraham is fulfilled in Jesus. The Gospel is for all nations, all peoples, all languages, and every person, regardless of ancestry or the degree of melanin their body produces. Let this message shine forth from every pulpit and pew. Take your children out of schools that divide students into groups of oppressors and oppressed, all while creating a hyper-sexualized environment. Attend only churches and schools that are clear about the universal sinfulness of the human race and uphold the

65 See Martin Luther, *Luther's Works*, American Edition, vol. 47, *The Christian in Society 4*, ed. Franklin Sherman and Helmut T. Lehmann (Philadelphia: Fortress Press, 1971), 123.

66 *Luther's Works*, vol. 47, 124.

67 For a refutation of this claim, see Uwe Siemon-Netto, *The Fabricated Luther: Refusing Nazi Connections and Other Myths*, 2nd ed. (St. Louis: Concordia Publishing House, 2007).

dignity and inherent value of every created human and teach the Gospel of Christ crucified and risen for all.

In the first part of this book, we have looked at the various social challenges to Christianity and seen how they all, from various angles, assault the order and purpose of God's creation. These are the disordered lies about the human race. In the second part of this book, we will first look at the benefits of Christ's work for the human race. He is the truth that sets us free. Then we will examine how you can apply these benefits in your own life to the challenges around you. And finally, we will conclude with the great hope of creation renewed.

REFLECTION QUESTIONS

1. How does CRT differ from the civil rights teachings of earlier generations?

2. How is public schooling different now than in previous generations?

3. How does the Bible describe the different ethnicities and languages in God's kingdom?

4. Why did God order the destruction of the Canaanites?

5. What is the source of divisions among nations?

6. How should Christians think about "race"?

7. How should Christians think about Jewish people?

PART II

HEALING HUMANITY

CHAPTER 8

MADE PERFECT THROUGH SUFFERING

Introduction

The healing of all humanity's ills that were first explored in Part I begins with Christ being made perfect. This immediately raises an objection: "Wasn't Christ perfect from His birth, even from all eternity?" This chapter explains why the Letter to the Hebrews says that Jesus was "made perfect through suffering." Recapitulating chapter 1, it demonstrates that man reaches his goal (*telos*) in Jesus. "Jesus . . . having loved His own who were in the world, . . . loved them to the end [*telos*]" (John 13:1). Jesus completes and brings to perfection the work of the true man in His death.

Christ Made Perfect

To be perfect is typically thought of as being without mistake or error. In baseball, a perfect game is when the pitcher allows no base-runners—no hits, walks, hit batters, or errors allowing a batter to reach base—for all nine innings. Likewise, in bowling, a perfect game is when every roll is a strike. No mistakes. This notion of perfection becomes confusing when we consider the passage from Hebrews that speaks of Christ being *made* perfect. "For it was fitting that He [God], for whom and by whom all things exist, in bringing many sons to glory, should make the founder of their salvation [i.e., Jesus] perfect[68] through suffering" (Hebrews 2:10). How can Jesus be made perfect, since He already was perfect—without error, without sin—from before His conception in Mary's womb?

This notion of perfection is not about being flawless but about taking something toward its ultimate purpose. John Kleinig observes that we should understand "made perfect" as "bringing someone to completion, so that he reached the goal that had been set for him."[69] So while the Son of God was flawless, morally perfect from all eternity, He had not yet accomplished in time the redemption of humanity. In the incarnation, the Second Person of the Trinity takes on a human body, assuming human nature into His person. The incarnate God-man endures every human difficulty—cold and heat, hunger and thirst, loneliness and forsakenness, betrayal and mockery, lies and scorn, suffering and death—without succumbing to temptation.

God is both source and goal of the created world. The incarnate God, Jesus, leads creation toward this goal in Himself. The Son of God takes mankind through death into glory. Crowned with glory and honor following His self-sacrifice, Jesus becomes the perfect man, that is, the man who has attained to what man was meant to be. This perfection could not be attained through the Old Testament priestly offerings. "Now if perfection had been attainable through the Levitical priesthood (for under it the people received the law), what further need would there have been for another priest to arise after the order of Melchizedek, rather than one named after the order of Aaron?" (Hebrews 7:11).

---

68 τελειῶσαι (teleiōsai). This verbal form of telos means to complete something, fulfilling it and bringing it to perfection. John Kleinig notes there is a play on words in this verse, contrasting "founder" (or "beginner") with "completion." See John W. Kleinig, Hebrews, Concordia Commentary (St. Louis: Concordia Publishing House, 2017), 120.

69 Kleinig, Hebrews, 145.

The Law anticipated the goal of Christ in the same way a shadow merely reflects the one casting it. "For since the law has but a shadow of the good things to come instead of the true form of these realities, it can never, by the same sacrifices that are continually offered every year, make perfect those who draw near" (Hebrews 10:1). This is why the works of the Law can never satisfy—perfect, bring to rest—a person's conscience (see Hebrews 9:9).

It is the new covenant in Christ's blood that makes perfect the conscience by distributing His holiness through the shed blood that forgives sins (see Matthew 26:27). Now in the perfection of His resurrection, He stands for us as our High Priest. The same blood by which He enters the Most Holy Place in heaven He distributes to us gathered to His Holy Communion. This blood, by absolving us of our sins, is working to make us perfect, as we are brought toward our goal of participation in "the resurrection of the body, and the life everlasting" (Apostles' Creed).

Man's Telos

That participation—or better, *communion*—in Christ's blood is your strength as you live toward the fulfillment of your own *telos,* your own goal. As we saw in the first chapter, God created man with a purpose. Although that purpose has been interrupted by the fall into corruption, man still has a purpose. Your individual life has meaning—not just for a future existence in the kingdom of God, but even now.

What is that purpose? Broadly speaking, God has given you a unique and particular calling through the time, place, and people He has put you with. The most wasted and foolish moments of my own life were those spent wishing I were with different people in a different place. Pastors sometimes wish they had a different church, where their current problems would be gone. The reality is that a different church would just have different problems—or maybe even the same—because people are still going to be sinners and the devil is still going to be at work. The same is true of wishing you had a different family or lived in a different time. But God has placed us in this time for this moment. The sooner we embrace that, the sooner we can begin moving toward the *telos* He has set for us, both in the work we are to do and the person we are to become.

I once heard a pastor explain how to understand the will of God by comparing it to children on a playground. Children are free to shoot baskets, slide down the slide, or swing on the swing set. There is no mysterious will of God that we are to mystically divine that will tell us we are to slide and not swing. We are free to do as we like; the world is our playground. However, the Ten Commandments govern our behavior on that playground. If I follow the Ten Commandments, I cannot grab the basketball from another child and kick it over the fence. That violates the Seventh Commandment, "You shall not steal." I cannot push someone off the swing, as that would violate the Fifth Commandment by hurting my neighbor. I cannot make fun of the person at the top of the slide who is afraid to go down, as that violates the Eighth Commandment, which governs sins of the tongue. I think this is a good analogy, and I often use it to guide people who wonder if they should take this job or that, move to this city or that.

However, the analogy is incomplete in many circumstances. That is because our existence in this world is not as individuals doing solitary things. God has placed us into a family, a church, and a community. We are born with parents, and often through those same parents, we have siblings and other extended relatives such as grandparents, uncles and aunts, and cousins. Later, through holy marriage, we are given a spouse and, as God wills, children. These relationships mean that we are not free to do whatever our personal desires dictate, but we need to care for the well-being of those God has placed in our families. To continue with the playground analogy, my desire to go down the slide must give way to my family's need for food, housing, medical care, spiritual care, education, and social/emotional support.

As our responsibilities expand, their demands start to come into conflict with one another. But especially, the demands conflict with our desires. One wants to spend time on the playground, but the needs of family, work, and church must take precedence. This can seem like suffering, but it really is simply maturation. This maturation as we embrace our responsibilities will look different for different people. For example, if you are a young man, it will likely mean that you put down the video game controller, get married, start a family, and quit squandering the life God gave you.

But then comes real suffering. Your parents age and need care. Your children struggle. Your health declines. Friends betray you. Even supposed brothers and sisters in Christ tell lies about you. And the world hates you. In addition to these sufferings comes the torment over your own sins. Is there any benefit to these sufferings?

The Benefit of Trials

Difficult to fathom, St. Paul nonetheless teaches us to glory in tribulations because of the fruit they bring forth. "We rejoice in our sufferings, knowing that suffering produces endurance, and endurance produces character, and character produces hope, and hope does not put us to shame, because God's love has been poured into our hearts through the Holy Spirit who has been given to us" (Romans 5:3–5). In the midst of sufferings, then, we confess that it is even God's kindness that is their cause because He wishes to produce within us an enduring hope and purity of heart. Luther says in his commentary on Romans, where he translates *suffering* as *trial*, "The expression 'trial' in this passage must be understood in a good sense, namely, as the goal of suffering, as that which is sought through tribulation. For God accepts no one as righteous whom He has not first tested, and He proves him through no other means than through the fire of tribulation, as we read in Ps. 17:3: 'Thou hast tried me by fire, and iniquity has not been found in me.'"[70] Some benefits to our faith and life that we receive through these trials are expanded upon below.

Chastening reveals the Father's love. The same theme is found in Hebrews. There the teacher shows us that God's chastisement is His way of training us as His sons. "'My son, do not regard lightly the discipline of the Lord, nor be weary when reproved by Him. For the Lord disciplines the one He loves, and chastises every son whom He receives.' It is for discipline that you have to endure. God is treating you as sons. For what son is there whom his father does not discipline?" (Hebrews 12:5–7).

Total dependence on grace. St. Paul pleaded with the Lord to remove his "thorn" from his flesh. What that "thorn" was is unknown. It could have been a physical malady, a temptation, or even a person or a demon since it is described as a messenger (angel) of Satan. I suspect the ambiguity is so that regardless of our difficulty, the Lord's response to Paul would apply also to us.

> So to keep me from becoming conceited because of
> the surpassing greatness of the revelations, a thorn

---

70 Martin Luther, *Luther's Works*, American Edition, vol. 25: *Lectures on Romans*, ed. Hilton C. Oswald (St. Louis: Concordia Publishing House, 1972), 291.

was given me in the flesh, a messenger of Satan to ha-
rass me, to keep me from becoming conceited. Three
times I pleaded with the Lord about this, that it should
leave me. But He said to me, "My grace is sufficient
for you, for My power is made perfect in weakness."
Therefore I will boast all the more gladly of my weaknesses, so that the power of Christ may rest upon me.
(2 Corinthians 12:7–9)

"My grace is sufficient for you." It is a diabolical delusion to
imagine that some created thing or some earthly circumstance is
needed. The only thing necessary is God's grace. If we have that,
then we have everything. If we lack His grace, then though we possess the entire world, we have nothing (see Matthew 16:26). Note
that the thorn in the flesh is actually a gift. God sent it to keep Paul
from being conceited. If you experienced great success, what might
it do to you? Might you become proud, complacent, and unrepen-
tant? In this way, God works even the assaults of the devil for your
good. Suffering causes you to recognize your own weakness, God's
strength, and especially His fatherly care for you. Deprivation of
worldly goods and success teaches you to realize that the kingdoms
of this earth are not truly valuable. Placing your hopes in them is
building houses on sand; when the great storm comes, the collapse
is catastrophic (see Matthew 7:24–27).

Union with Christ. Christians who suffer for the sake of Christ's
name (i.e., His Word and doctrine) and endure the world's scorn
for faithfulness to Him are given special promises. "The Spirit Himself bears witness with our spirit that we are children of God, and
if children, then heirs—heirs of God and fellow heirs with Christ,
provided we suffer with Him in order that we may also be glorified
with Him" (Romans 8:16–17). Suffering here *for* Christ's sake is

also said to be suffering *with* Him. We join Him in His suffering, although it is better to think of it the other way around: Christ stands with us and strengthens us in the hour of trial, for we are members of His Body.

We ought not to wish for martyrdom in a masochistic way. Nevertheless, suffering for the sake of Christ's name is spoken of in Scripture as a precious gift. St. Paul spoke this way to the Philippians as they contended for the Gospel: "It has been granted to you that for the sake of Christ you should not only believe in Him but also suffer for His sake" (Philippians 1:29). Contrary to much of contemporary American Christianity, which sees financial prosperity, health, and worldly success as marks of God's favor, the Scriptures teach us that fidelity to Jesus will bring suffering. "Indeed, all who desire to live a godly life in Christ Jesus will be persecuted" (2 Timothy 3:12).

Years ago, a friend of mine, a pastor, came to me to discuss how he had been horribly mistreated by another pastor. The results were potentially catastrophic, and his fear and anger were palpable. The words still ring in my ears: "I expected the world to persecute me. I didn't expect it from the church." In such occasions, it is beneficial to remember that Jesus' betrayer was one of His own disciples. The actions of Judas are prophesied in the Psalms: "Even my close friend in whom I trusted, who ate my bread, has lifted his heel against me" (Psalm 41:9). Jesus said that we would find enemies in our own households (see Matthew 10:36; cf. Micah 7:6). This is certainly going to be true of the church as well. St. Paul complains by name about those who caused him harm, even uttering imprecations (see 2 Timothy 4:14).

While St. Paul may call down judgment upon a person, I don't feel comfortable with doing the same. Perhaps I should have that confidence, but I am no apostle, and I am acutely aware of my own failings when others, even within the church, have turned upon me and become my enemies. One of the most useful things for me to realize was to take seriously the command to pray for our enemies (Matthew 5:44).

For too long, it seemed like a sin in itself to name someone before God as my enemy. But there are two circumstances for someone becoming my enemy: either through my own action or through the other person's. If it is mine, then praying for that person forces me to reflect before the throne of God on what I have done to cause the rift. In such a circumstance, the Word of God calls me to go to the person and confess: "So if you are offering your gift at the altar and there remember that your brother has something against you, leave your gift there before the altar and go. First be reconciled to your brother, and then come and offer your gift" (Matthew 5:23–24). But if the person has something against me without a cause, then naming him as my enemy is not an act of malice but a recognition of the broken situation. Instead of seething with anger, I invite God into the relationship to work, if it is His will, restoration. And if that is not possible, then I ask for the gift of patience and love, knowing that it is only by grace that I am no longer counted as God's enemy.

This recognition that God has declared friendship toward His enemies must work to change my heart, to be ready to forgive those who hate me. "For if while we were enemies we were reconciled to God by the death of His Son, much more, now that we are reconciled, shall we be saved by His life. More than that, we also rejoice in God through our Lord Jesus Christ, through whom we have now received reconciliation" (Romans 5:10–11).

Afflictions drive us to the Word. Wilhelm Löhe was a German

pastor responsible for great mission work in the United States while faithfully pastoring his congregation in Neuendettelsau, Germany. This is his important counsel in the face of trouble: "Trust his Word: do not stray from it. Whatever temptation, perplexity, or feelings a man may encounter, let him continually retain the sharp distinction between God and man, between God's Word and feelings, between God's faithfulness and man's opinions; let him stand on faith and press on with the unconditioned, unemotional faith that depends only on the Word."[71]

Healing

In the ministry of Jesus, the body was not secondary. It is tempting to "spiritualize" the work of Jesus so that His healing of bodies is seen entirely as a metaphor for something spiritual. The body and soul are connected by God's creative act; they hang together in a constitutive reality. "The day that you eat of it you shall surely die" (Genesis 2:17) indicates that sin affects both body and soul, an idea reiterated by St. Paul's statement, "The wages of sin is death" (Romans 6:23). Jesus demonstrates this connection with the healing of the paralytic:

> And behold, some people brought to Him a paralytic, lying on a bed. And when Jesus saw their faith, He said to the paralytic, "Take heart, My son; your sins are forgiven." And behold, some of the scribes said to themselves, "This man is blaspheming." But Jesus, knowing their thoughts, said, "Why do you think evil in your hearts? For which is easier, to say, 'Your sins are forgiven,' or to say, 'Rise and walk'? But that you

---

71   J. K. Wilhelm Löhe, *The Word Remains: Selected Writings on the Church Year and the Christian Life* (Fort Wayne, IN: Emmanuel Press, 2016), 81.

may know that the Son of Man has authority on earth to forgive sins"—He then said to the paralytic—"Rise, pick up your bed and go home." And he rose and went home. When the crowds saw it, they were afraid, and they glorified God, who had given such authority to men. (Matthew 9:2–7)

The forgiveness of sins and the healing of the body are intrinsically linked because the soul and the body are intrinsically linked. This is a point made in both the Apostles' and the Nicene Creeds, which confess "the forgiveness of sins, and the resurrection of the body" (Apostles' Creed) and "one Baptism for the remission of sins, and I look for the resurrection of the dead and the life of the world to come" (Nicene Creed).[72]

Sacraments are embodied acts that declare the same thing, connecting the healing of the soul to the transformation of the body. The Christian faith is not a set of moral prescriptions. The Gospel is for the healing of the human person. The repentant sinner approaches Jesus not to receive His techniques for an improved lifestyle but for union with Him who liberates the world from its bondage to corruption.

Incarnation and Ascension

The work of Jesus is incomprehensible apart from the body. The writer to the Hebrews puts Psalm 40 on the lips of the incarnate Christ: "Consequently, when Christ came into the world, He said, 'Sacrifices and offerings You have not desired, but a body have You prepared for Me'" (Hebrews 10:5). That the Second Person of the Holy Trinity took on a body changes everything for everybody. He was subject to the Law in His body, beginning with His

---

72 *LSB*, pp. 158–59.

circumcision. In His ascension, He entered with His body into the heavenly Most Holy Place, with His blood an eternal, perpetual sacrifice that brings to an end the sacrifices of bulls and goats. In the incarnate Son, God was made man, and in Him, man is deified.

The implications of this are breathtaking. Man is not meant to slough off his body to become an incorporeal being. For man was not meant to die. The resurrection of Jesus is the victory of humanity in Him over death. That victory He shares with His disciples. The beginnings thereof are bestowed in Holy Baptism, as St. Paul writes:

> Do you not know that all of us who have been baptized into Christ Jesus were baptized into His death? We were buried therefore with Him by baptism into death, in order that, just as Christ was raised from the dead by the glory of the Father, we too might walk in newness of life. For if we have been united with Him in a death like His, we shall certainly be united with Him in a resurrection like His. (Romans 6:3–5)

As Baptism is corporeal—the application of water to the body as the Word, the triune name, is spoken—so this resurrection is corporeal. This is no metaphor; the body of the disciple is raised, just as the body of Jesus is risen from the dead, and will live to all eternity.

Now elsewhere, St. Paul does describe this as a "spiritual" body. What does this mean? The body, he writes, "is sown in dishonor; it is raised in glory. It is sown in weakness; it is raised in power. It is sown a natural body; it is raised a spiritual body. If there is a natural body, there is also a spiritual body" (1 Corinthians 15:43–44). Many people in our modern age have become captivated by the idea that *spiritual* means "nonphysical." However, the Bible frequently uses the distinction between *flesh* and *spirit* not to mean "physical" and "immaterial" but to mean "enslaved to sin" over against being led by God's Spirit. Some Bible and catechism translations even render *flesh* as "sinful nature," such as in the common phrase "the devil, the world, and our sinful nature" (vs. "the devil, the world, and our flesh"[73]). We should not understand St. Paul as saying *spiritual* means not having a material body. Instead, it means having a body not filled with the corruption of the sinful nature. The spiritual body is in fact a body, but one animated fully by the Holy Spirit. This supernatural work will make the resurrected Christian have a body that "is the perfect dwelling and instrument of the Spirit."[74]

The resurrected Jesus had a body that could be touched (John 20:27) and could eat (Luke 24:39–43). This is a body that is material and yet fully spiritual—or better, *Spiritual*, as this man is the One in whom the Holy Spirit has found again a home among man. What will be fully the case in the resurrection of all those who believe in Christ is breaking even now into this world among the faithful. On the evening of His resurrection, Jesus breathed on His disciples and caused them to receive the Holy Spirit (John 20:22). That gift enabled the disciples to forgive and retain sins—which is the continuing work of the Holy Spirit in the world—as they preach the Gospel to all nations. That preaching produces repentance leading to Baptism, which gives both the gift of the Holy Spirit and the remission of sins (Acts 2:38). The Holy Spirit dwells in the disciple of Jesus not only in the heart but also in the body. Thus, as a body is washed with water in Baptism and fed with the body and blood of Jesus, the entire human person is being sanctified in preparation for the full transformation of the resurrection.

---

73   E.g., the explanation of the Third and Sixth Petitions in Luther's Small Catechism (St. Louis: Concordia Publishing House, 1986).

74   Walter H. Roehrs and Martin H. Franzmann, *Concordia Self-Study Commentary*, (St. Louis: Concordia Publishing House, 1971, 1979), 158.

Conclusion

Christ became incarnate for the purpose of healing our nature. Morally perfect from all eternity, He took our nature into His person and brought it to its goal. In Him is both divine and human perfection. Our sins are forgiven, and the process of perfection is working out in us now as we suffer, renounce the devil's lies, and cling to Christ, the perfect One. His healing addresses everything corrupt within us, a therapeutic remedy even for the deepest disorders of our nature.

REFLECTION QUESTIONS

1. What does it mean that Jesus was "made perfect"?

2. How does Jesus use His own blood?

3. What is man's purpose?

4. What are the benefits of suffering?

5. How should we deal with our enemies?

6. What is the connection between sin and the body?

7. What is the proper distinction between flesh and spirit?

8. What is God planning for our bodies?

CHAPTER 9

CONVERSION THERAPY

Introduction

The LGBTQ movement has anathematized the idea of "conversion therapy," which seeks to heal those struggling with aberrant sexual desires. Building on the foundation laid in previous chapters, this chapter focuses on every person's need for conversion: conversion from spiritual death to faith in Christ, and ongoing conversion therapy to heal the innate lusts the believer still struggles with. Baptism is the foundational sacrament of conversion, with a lifelong application.

Conversion Controversy

Among LGBTQ propagandists, conversion therapy is an umbrella term that describes any spiritual or mental health counseling that begins from the teaching that LGBTQ behaviors are abnormal. Attempts to make "conversion therapy" illegal are rooted in the ultimate goal of suppressing and eradicating Christianity and its doctrine that sexuality finds its proper arena within holy marriage between one man and one woman. In early 2022, for example, the West Lafayette (Indiana) city council proposed an ordinance banning conversion therapy that would make it illegal for an adult to speak with minors who want to overcome a same-sex attraction or gender dysphoria. Such bans could have the effect of silencing preaching and pastoral care based on the teaching of Holy Scripture about the meaning and purpose of human nature and sexuality. It could even potentially criminalize parents who teach their children God's purpose for their bodies. The city council later dropped the ban proposal, opting to instead "condemn" the practice.[75] The trend nevertheless is toward the silencing of anyone who would uphold the biblical worldview of the human person and the purpose of traditional marriage and the sexual relationship between husband and wife.

It is important for Christians to recognize that conversion therapy, narrowly defined, is highly questionable. It comes from the psychotherapeutic worldview that does not affirm the biblical doctrine of original sin nor account for grace and the intervention of the Holy Spirit. Beginning with a humanistic approach to the person, conversion therapy, also known as reparative therapy, seeks by the discipline of psychology to change a person's sexual orientation—sexual impulses or desires—or "gender identity." As we have seen, our impulses in a Christian understanding stem from the brokenness of the human person—concupiscence, the passions. One cannot psychologize these away. Past methods of conversion therapy allegedly included the use of drugs to induce nausea, repeated exposure to pornography, electroshock treatments, undressing, separation from family, and sexual experimentation with the opposite sex.[76]

Joseph Nicolosi, author of *Reparative Therapy of Male Homosexuality: A New Clinical Approach*[77] and founder of the National Association for Research and Therapy for Homosexuality (NARTH), rejected the association of reparative therapy with

---

75   Margaret Christopherson, "West Lafayette Leaders Condemn Conversion Therapy, Withdraw Proposed Ban," *Lafayette Journal and Courier*, February 7, 2022, https://www.jconline.com/story/news/2022/02/07/conversion-therapy-west-lafayette-council-condemns-pull-proposed-ban/6698052001/.

76   See Joe Dallas, *Speaking of Homosexuality: Discussing the Issues with Kindness and Clarity* (Grand Rapids, MI: Baker Books, 2016), 81.

77   Published by Jason Aronson, 1991.

conversion therapy. Nicolosi's approach was not biblical, but psychotherapeutic, utilizing the history of psychoanalysis, including Freud. He grounded his research on childhood experiences of shame and the failure to receive love and support from male role models. He believed that family and social influences shape a person's sexual desires, not biology. Nicolosi specifically rejected coercion. His reparative therapy is only for those who wish to address their desires and not be defined by homosexuality. While largely discredited, Nicolosi's work is still recognized by some such as Joe Dallas, a prominent author and speaker on homosexuality and Christianity.[78]

Dallas cautions that the term "reparative therapy" should be confined to licensed therapists who apply psychological approaches such as NARTH's in a clinical practice.[79] In his counseling practice, he believes the treatment of those struggling with same-sex attraction should focus on a change of behavior. Furthermore, the person should reject homosexuality as an identity; a person is more than his or her (often sinful) desires. While temptations often continue, they can be resisted. Emotional attraction to those of the opposite sex is the beginning of a rightly ordered attraction, although the sexual attraction may never be as strong as it was toward the same sex. Dallas argues that, even though most psychological and medical associations have become pro-LGBTQ, it is unfair and unethical to not give traditionally minded people, including Christians, access to the therapeutic help they are seeking.[80]

Converting Desire

How should we think about desires that we have—sexual or otherwise—that we would like to change or gain freedom from?

---

78 Dallas, *Speaking of Homosexuality*, 84.
79 Dallas, *Speaking of Homosexuality*, 85.
80 Dallas, *Speaking of Homosexuality*, 85–86.

We cannot change our desires on our own any more than we can cause ourselves to be born—or reborn. Since the fall into sin, human nature is hostile to God. St. Paul describes it as dead:

> You were dead in the trespasses and sins in which you once walked, following the course of this world, following the prince of the power of the air, the spirit that is now at work in the sons of disobedience—among whom we all once lived in the passions of our flesh, carrying out the desires of the body and the mind, and were by nature children of wrath, like the rest of mankind. (Ephesians 2:1–3)

This condition of spiritual death means each human person is a slave to desire, consumed by the passions. It is impossible to change this condition ourselves. The transformation is the work of God, as St. Paul says shortly after: "But God, being rich in mercy, . . . even when we were dead in our trespasses, made us alive together with Christ" (Ephesians 2:4–5). Yet, while this new spiritual birth from the dead means a change of status before God—the newborn soul is justified (declared righteous) before God—the Christian nevertheless is called to growth. Later in that Letter to the Ephesians, Paul exhorts the newborn to "walk in a manner worthy of the calling to which you have been called" (Ephesians 4:1) with an aim to maturation: "So that we may no longer be children. . . . Rather, speaking the truth in love, we are to grow up in every way into Him who is the head, into Christ" (Ephesians 4:14–15).

What Paul describes as growth from newborn to mature, Jesus describes as healing. The parable of the Good Samaritan (Luke 10:25–37) demonstrates how Christ, after regeneration, begins to heal our nature. The parable is often described in a moralistic sense, as though the message is that we should help other people in need. Certainly, we should; the commandment to love our neighbors as ourselves (Luke 10:27) enjoins us to this very thing. But the parable is not about helping others; it is about our need for help.

The object of the parable is "man," a man who falls prey to bandits who beat him to the edge of death, rob him of his goods, strip him of his clothing, and leave him at the side of the road. Often characters in the parables of Jesus have a descriptor that helps with the meaning: a king, a bridegroom, a steward, a sheep, and such. In this case, the lack of a descriptor is important: the man left for dead is *man*, mankind, *anthrōpos* (the generic Greek word for human being, not specifically a male or female). We can picture this man as Adam: turning from God's Word (going down from the city of God, Jerusalem, to the city of man, Jericho), he discovers he is naked, robbed of his original righteousness, exiled from Eden, dying. This man is Adam—and us, all of mankind.

The Law, represented by the priest and the Levite, cannot rescue man, only Jesus can. Jesus is represented by the Samaritan in the parable. He steps in and picks up man from his ditch. Caring for man's wounds, He pours on oil and wine to disinfect and soothe. But man is still in danger. Luther describes it this way:

> To be sure, the wounds of the half-dead man have been bound up, as the parable in Luke 10:34 states. Oil and wine have been poured on them, and the gift of the Holy Spirit has begun. Nevertheless, the wounds are still deadly. Care has been taken to heal him. But he has not yet been completely restored. If you should want to say that there is no wound, that there is no danger, find out whether a half-dead man can walk, work, and do what a healthy man can do. He is carried

by the beast on which he has been placed. He does not work; he does not walk. Thus through Baptism we have been taken upon God's beast, that is, the most precious sacrifice for us, or the humanity of Christ, by which we are carried. Although we have been accepted once, yet we are cared for and healed from day to day.[81]

In other words, Baptism delivers to us the verdict of justification and gives to us the new birth of the Holy Spirit, but the work of healing continues. The conclusion of the parable has the Samaritan leaving behind two valuable coins for the man's healing, promising to provide whatever else is needed for his ongoing care. From the point of rescue to the final perfection, the work is delivered to man from the outside. The Samaritan—Christ—is continually healing us, working purification and sanctification within us.[82]

What this means for you is that however your struggles with sin manifest themselves, you are not uniquely depraved. You are not beyond redemption. You are not beyond healing. "No temptation has overtaken you that is not common to man" (1 Corinthians 10:13). All of humanity is together in the ditch, needing to be rescued from the outside. All of humanity is together on the mortician's slab, needing revivification. This applies to you as an individual. This applies to your daughter, son, brother, and neighbor. None of us can save ourselves. None of us can heal ourselves. Christ, our Good Samaritan, comes to us in our ditch. To porn addicts and church gossips, temper-losers and abortion providers, same-sex and opposite-sex fornicators, husband-divorcers and wife-abusers, drunkards and gluttons—to all of these Christ comes. Every other

---

81 Martin Luther, *Luther's Works*, American Edition, vol. 7, *Lectures on Genesis Chapters 38–44*, ed. Jaroslav Pelikan and Walter A. Hansen, trans. Paul D. Pahl (St. Louis: Concordia Publishing House, 1965), 281–82.

82 See Martin Luther, *Luther's Works*, American Edition, vol. 41, *Church and Ministry 3*, ed. Eric W. Gritsch and Helmut T. Lehmann (Philadelphia: Fortress Press, 1966), 218.

way we humans find to degrade and destroy ourselves is simply a variation on the bandits who have bruised and battered us, leaving us half-dead. For you and every sinner, Christ has come, both to declare you righteous and to heal you from every unrighteousness.

In His work of healing, Jesus is liberating you from the things that bind and enslave you. He accomplishes this by the same means that deliver justification to you: His Holy Word and the Sacraments. It is tempting to think of sin purely as negative marks that need to be erased, a kind of debit in an account that needs to be brought back to a positive balance. There is some benefit to thinking of justification this way. We find that kind of language in Genesis 15:6, where Abram "believed the LORD, and He counted it to him as righteousness." Here, Scripture describes justification as a legal or financial counting. At the same time, we see in the language of Scripture the power of sin to wound the soul. The Means of Grace, when received in faith, deliver the judicial verdict and also effect healing.

Baptism is one such healing, and it begins God's work of transformation. It works a new birth and recreates the heart, which rejoices in God's Commandments. Luther's 1523 "Order of Baptism" sees this foundational Sacrament as a transition from unholy to holy desires, praying for the one about to be baptized:

> Drive away from him all the blindness of his heart, break all the snares of the devil with which he is bound, open to him, Lord, the door of thy grace: So that marked with the sign of thy wisdom he may be free of the stench of all evil lusts and serve thee joyfully according to the sweet savor of thy commandments in thy church and grow daily.[83]

---

83   Martin Luther, *Luther's Works*, American Edition, Vol. 53, *Liturgy and Hymns*, ed. Ulrich S. Leupold and

This is a radically different heart from the one who sees desire as something to be embraced. Desires (evil lusts), so pleasant to fallen man, are revealed to have a foul stench. From the womb, they blind and enslave man. Liberty is not in following those natural desires but in the action of Christ, who breaks the snares, illumines the mind, opens the door of grace, and places man on a new path toward growth.

The Lord's Supper, also, can rightly be spoken of as having a bodily benefit. This can be inferred from the bodily danger of eating unworthily, which can even cause death (1 Corinthians 11:27–30). The dismissal formula in *Lutheran Service Book* speaks of a bodily benefit for the communicants: "The body and blood of our Lord Jesus Christ strengthen and preserve you in body and soul to life everlasting. Depart in peace."[84] While what bodily benefits the Lord's Supper may have in temporal life remain a mystery, it certainly points toward the resurrection of the body. Luther hints at this in his great treatise "That These Words of Christ, 'This Is My Body,' Etc., Still Stand Firm against the Fanatics":

> Irenaeus and the ancient fathers pointed out the benefit that our body is fed with the body of Christ, in order that our faith and hope may abide and that our body also may live eternally from the same eternal food of the body of Christ which it eats physically. This is a bodily benefit, nevertheless an extraordinarily great one, and it follows from the spiritual benefit. For Christ surely will make even our body eternal, alive, blessed, and glorious, which is a much greater thing than giving us his body to eat for a short time

Helmut T. Lehmann (Philadelphia: Fortress Press, 1965), 96.
84   *LSB*, p. 164.

on earth. Therefore he wills to be "in us by nature," says Hilary, in both our soul and body, according to the word in John 6[:56], "He who eats me abides in me and I in him." If we eat him spiritually through the Word, he abides in us spiritually in our soul; if one eats him physically, he abides in us physically and we in him. As we eat him, he abides in us and we in him. For he is not digested or transformed but ceaselessly he transforms us, our soul into righteousness, our body into immortality. So the ancient fathers spoke of the physical eating.[85]

One practice of ancient use in the sacramental piety of the Church is to pray for the soul's healing when receiving the Lord's body and blood. Consider the response of the centurion in Capernaum when Jesus offered to come to his home to heal his servant: "Lord, I am not worthy to have You come under my roof, but only say the word, and my servant will be healed" (Matthew 8:8). This has become a model prayer before receiving the host. Many use an altered form of this prayer when preparing to receive the Eucharist: "Lord, I am not worthy that Thou shouldst enter under my roof, but speak only Thy Word, and my soul shall be healed."

Regenerate Sex

In a previous chapter, we saw that the popularization of Freud's ideas moved sex from activity to identity. The healing of humanity that takes place within the Holy Christian Church on earth will convert the way husbands and wives understand their sexual intimacy.

---

85   Martin Luther, *Luther's Works*, American Edition, vol. 37, *Word and Sacrament 3*, ed. Robert H. Fischer and Helmut T. Lehmann (Philadelphia: Fortress Press, 1961), 132.

The Scriptures discuss sex within holy marriage in numerous ways. Sex is for the following:

Personal intimacy. "Now Adam knew Eve his wife, and she conceived and bore Cain" (Genesis 4:1). This is not a euphemism, as in the sexual union, Adam knows Eve as a complete person. The verb "to know" signifies that in their sexual intercourse, they were united as one flesh and also united in heart and mind.

Procreation. The previous passage connects the intimate knowledge of each other in intercourse with the conception of a child. Regenerate sex is open to life. Common objections to this, such as "We're not ready for children," "We have to finish school first," "We want to wait for a while and just enjoy ourselves," and, "We can't afford it yet" are all rooted in personal ambition, which places human will over God's will. "What God has joined together, let no one put asunder."[86] God has joined intercourse to procreation. Yet even many healthy couples make great efforts to separate the two. What this does is place pleasure and money ahead of God's will. Children are seen as curses if they do not come at a time of our choosing. Yet God's Word universally describes children as a blessing, not a curse. Eve rejoiced at the birth of her son: "Now Adam knew Eve his wife, and she conceived and bore Cain, saying, 'I have gotten a man with the help of the Lord'" (Genesis 4:1). Although Cain did not fulfill her desires for him, Eve rightly saw him as a gift from the Lord. Solomon is more explicit: "Behold, children are a heritage from the Lord, the fruit of the womb a reward. Like arrows in the hand of a warrior are the children of one's youth. Blessed is the man who fills his quiver with them!" (Psalm 127:3–5). The subsequent psalm extends this description of blessing to a rich home and family life extending to multiple generations for

---

86   *LSB,* p. 277.

the man who fears Yahweh: "Your wife will be like a fruitful vine within your house; your children will be like olive shoots around your table. Behold, thus shall the man be blessed who fears the LORD. The LORD bless you from Zion! May you see the prosperity of Jerusalem all the days of your life! May you see your children's children! Peace be upon Israel!" (Psalm 128:3–6).

Protection against temptation. St. Paul expects that Christians will practice the discipline of abstinence (i.e., fasting from food and refraining from sexual activity). Yet he cautions husbands and wives not to withhold themselves sexually from each other outside of these agreed-upon times of abstinence.

> Because of the temptation to sexual immorality, each man should have his own wife and each woman her own husband. The husband should give to his wife her conjugal rights, and likewise the wife to her husband. For the wife does not have authority over her own body, but the husband does. Likewise the husband does not have authority over his own body, but the wife does. Do not deprive one another, except perhaps by agreement for a limited time, that you may devote yourselves to prayer; but then come together again, so that Satan may not tempt you because of your lack of self-control. (1 Corinthians 7:2–5)

In the same passage, while he commends those who remain single (possibly because of the crisis in Corinth),[87] he advises those with strong sexual desires to marry so they may avoid sin: "But if

---

87 St. Paul's advice about remaining in one's current state (whether married or unmarried) is given "in view of the present distress" (1 Corinthians 7:26). There is some hardship that has come upon the Corinthians that Paul has in view, possibly a famine. The advice that Paul gives, therefore, about it being good to remain unmarried, should be viewed as highly contextual and not generally applicable. See Leon Morris, *1 Corinthians: An Introduction and Commentary*, Tyndale New Testament Commentaries, vol. 7 (Downers Grove, IL: InterVarsity Press, 1985), 115.

they cannot exercise self-control, they should marry. For it is better to marry than to burn with passion" (1 Corinthians 7:9).

Conclusion

The gift of sexual intimacy is intended for holy marriage. The profoundly deleterious effects of concupiscence catastrophically altered our ability to use this gift without sin. Everyone, regardless of individual proclivities and orientations, needs conversion and healing in both sexual relations and other things that deeply affect the soul. The desires we feel so strongly are called in classical Christian spirituality "the passions." Should you follow your passion(s)? The next chapter will address that question.

REFLECTION QUESTIONS

1. How is conversion therapy variously defined? How should Christians think about it?

2. How should people who want their desires changed be helped?

3. What does the parable of the Good Samaritan teach us about man and Christ?

4. How do the sacraments of Holy Baptism and the Lord's Supper heal us?

5. How should we think about sex within holy marriage?

CHAPTER 10

DON'T FOLLOW YOUR PASSIONS

Introduction

The popular slogan "Follow your passion" is terrible advice for the Christian. Jesus calls His disciples to fight their passions. Passion leads us to sin, and "the wages of sin is death" (Romans 6:23). In the previous chapter, we identified the need for healing, especially in the area of sexuality. This chapter broadens that theme, showing how the passions affect many areas of our life. As part of our self-examination (1 Corinthians 11:28), we disciples of Jesus are called to identify the passions burning within us and then pray for the Holy Spirit's help for the discipline to overcome the temptations the passions present.

Passion Is Suffering

We saw previously that the word *hedonism* is derived from the Greek term for *pleasure* (*hēdonē*), the desire for which enslaves man. In James 4:1–3, the ESV translation helpfully renders the term as *passions*: "What causes quarrels and what causes fights among you? Is it not this, that your passions are at war within you? You desire and do not have, so you murder. You covet and cannot obtain, so you fight and quarrel. You do not have, because you do not ask. You ask and do not receive, because you ask wrongly, to spend it on your passions."

"Passion" is a popular term today, including among Christians. It is properly used to describe the suffering and death of Jesus. Thus the accounts in the Gospels for Holy Thursday and Good Friday are typically called, for example, "The Passion according to St. Matthew." The English word *passion* is derived from the Latin word for suffering. That is also what "the passions" (in the negative sense) do to the human soul: they both stem from and cause suffering.

Classical Christian spirituality sought to identify and strengthen resistance to these passions. Intertestamental works take up the question about how godly reason might rule over these passions by highlighting virtues like self-control, justice (righteousness), and courage opposed to gluttony, lust, malice, anger, fear, and pain. Other Christian ascetical texts have related lists, such as *gluttony, avarice*, and *seeking the esteem of men* in the first group, followed by *unchastity, anger, dejection*, and *pride*.[88] In this latter rendering, the passions of the first group lead to those in the second. For example, excess in eating (gluttony) leads to a loss of self-control of other bodily desires, such as the desire for sex outside of holy marriage (unchastity). Gluttony, avarice, and seeking the esteem of men are seen as parallels to the temptation of Jesus after His forty-day fast (Matthew 4:1–11). Gluttony corresponds to the temptation to turn stones into bread, avarice corresponds to possessing the kingdoms of the world, and the esteem of men corresponds to the expected result of Jesus flying through the air off the pinnacle of the temple, caught by angels, and then praised by those who beheld it.

Discipline for the Passions

The exhortation of Jesus that certain demons are expelled only

---

88 See, for example, St. John Cassian, "On Eight Vices," in the *Philokalia* or in *On the Institutes of the Coenobia and the Remedies for the Eight Principal Faults*, Books 5–12, in *A Select Library of Nicene and Post-Nicene Fathers of the Christian Church*, Second Series, vol. 11, ed. Philip Schaff and Henry Wace (Edinburgh: T&T Clark; reprinted in Grand Rapids, MI: William B. Eerdmans Publishing Company, 1964).

through fasting and prayer (Matthew 17:21) is connected to the Sermon on the Mount's exhortation to give ourselves to fasting, prayer, and almsgiving (Matthew 6:1–18). These spiritual disciplines are the tools God has given us to battle the passions. While Lent has a special focus on these disciplines, the whole Christian life is intended to be dedicated to them.

Forty: The Number of Journey

The three temptations of Jesus mentioned above are connected with the highly charged number forty: "After fasting forty days and forty nights, He [Jesus] was hungry" (Matthew 4:1). In Scripture, the number forty is used for journey or passage—it symbolizes movement from death to life. During the flood, Noah was in the ark while it rained for forty days and forty nights. Moses fasted on Mount Sinai for forty days and forty nights when he received the Ten Commandments. Israel wandered in the wilderness for forty years. Elijah received food from God and journeyed on the strength of that food for forty days and forty nights. All those events are wrapped up in Jesus, who sets out on the ultimate journey on behalf of all our human race.

Feasting and fasting. These journeys are connected to another significant scriptural theme: feasting and fasting. The Lord proclaimed for Adam and Eve a continual feast, "You may surely eat of every tree of the garden" (Genesis 2:16). Yet the only command God gave was a command to fast, "But of the tree of the knowledge of good and evil you shall not eat, for in the day that you eat of it you shall surely die" (Genesis 2:17). Not content with the feast that God had provided, Adam and Eve chose to break the fast, giving in to temptation. Theirs was a journey from the feasting in the garden to toil and labor just to get bread: "Cursed is the ground because of you; in pain you shall eat of it all the days of your life; thorns and thistles it shall bring forth for you; and you shall eat the plants of the field. By the sweat of your face you shall eat bread" (Genesis 3:17–19).

Temptations assault our weaknesses. We are people who give in to temptation over and over and over again. The tempter knows that the way to our soul and spirit is through the passions of our body. St. Paul speaks in Philippians 3 of the enemies of Christ: "Their end is destruction, their god is their belly" (v.19). Man fell by breaking the fast, and so lost the feast God prepared for him. In His temptation, Jesus undoes the tempter's work by not breaking His fast. Matthew understates it, telling us Jesus was hungry. But He must have been near death. Who can go without food and water for even a day without bellyaching? At the moment Jesus is weakest, after a forty-day fast, the devil chooses to attack. "If You are the Son of God, command these stones to become loaves of bread" (Matthew 4:3).

The devil always attacks us at our weakest points. In such a circumstance, we make giving in to temptation so reasonable. We are quick to rationalize our sin, explaining to ourselves all the extenuating circumstances that allow us to break God's Law and do what we want.

The Devil Hates the Baptized

Temptation comes right on the heels of Baptism. The narrative of Jesus' temptation begins with the little word *then*: "Then Jesus was led up by the Spirit into the wilderness to be tempted by the devil" (Matthew 4:1). Immediately preceding this, John baptized Jesus. Applying this to ourselves, we see that the devil tempts the baptized. Your Baptism angers and enrages the devil. You no longer belong to him but to God, who has put His name on you. So the devil tries to make you reject your Baptism by turning you away from dependence upon God back into the love of self. He exploits your passions. The devil attacks you where you are weak.

Where are you weak? At that spot, you will be tempted. For each of us, the temptation is different, and it can change over time. The remedy for our passions is daily, constant use of the Word of God and prayer based upon it.

The Lord Jesus overcame temptation by means of the Word of God. With each of Satan's temptations in the wilderness, Jesus, the Word made flesh, answered the tempter with the scriptural Word. "Man shall not live by bread alone, but by every word that comes from the mouth of God" (Matthew 4:4). While some might urge you to rely on your own self-control, it is only the Word and the Spirit, help from the outside, that can give you godly self-control.

The three disciplines. The three disciplines exercise every part of us. Fasting disciplines the body, prayer exercises the spirit by speaking back to God what He has said to us, and almsgiving (or works of mercy) trains us to put our neighbor ahead of ourselves. Jesus gives us these disciplines to help us battle the passions. Controlling your body by fasting counteracts gluttony and sexual immorality. Focusing on praying God's Word back to God combats unbelief and misbelief. Training your eyes to focus on the needs of others through almsgiving helps you defeat rage, anger, meanness, and pride. These disciplines to control the passions show us that being disciples of Jesus is a matter of the whole life, not simply a matter of assent to certain intellectual statements of doctrine.

Adam and Eve broke the fast God had commanded, and so they lost the feast God had given. Learning to fast, pray, and be kind prepares us to enjoy and celebrate fully what God has given us now. These disciplines also move the heart, increasing its reliance on God's mercy instead of indulging the passions, in anticipation of the joy and feasting of the resurrection.

Grace to Help in Time of Need

God does not leave you to overcome your passions alone. That is impossible. Victory over passions is possible only by the Holy Spirit. He gives us what He requires. Christian discipline begins with acknowledging our passions and how much they have controlled us. Only when we see that we are weak does the Lord give us His strength. "For we do not have a high priest who is unable to sympathize with our weaknesses, but one who in every respect has been tempted as we are, yet without sin. Let us then with confidence draw near to the throne of grace, that we may receive mercy and find grace to help in time of need" (Hebrews 4:15–16). Jesus is sympathetic, which is to say He suffers with us. When you are feeling that the passions are too strong for you, run to confession, run to the Word, run to the Eucharist. There Jesus joins His body to earthly bread by means of His Word. He Himself is our food for the journey. He who overcame and defeated the passions Himself will also defeat them within you. "No temptation has overtaken you that is not common to man. God is faithful, and He will not let you be tempted beyond your ability, but with the temptation He will also provide the way of escape, that you may be able to endure it" (1 Corinthians 10:13). Whatever challenges you face may feel unique, but they are shared by others. You are not alone.

You are not defined by your feelings. Most significantly, your passions are not your identity! Our age is identity-crazed, where you are encouraged to identify with various groups and especially find your identity in your sexual passions. You do not have to live that way. That is not how God sees you. Don't identify yourself by your passions but by who God says you are: His beloved child. Whatever you have done, whatever you feel, His Word trumps it. His identity is yours. Read the Word He spoke over Jesus at His Baptism: "This is My beloved Son, with whom I am well pleased" (Matthew 3:17). Now insert your own name into it and hear the Father's voice saying to you, "You are My beloved child, with whom I am well pleased." That "well pleased" is entirely grace. You have not earned it. An identity derived from your passions is beneath your humanity. The Lord makes you His child through adoption into His people through your Baptism (see Galatians 4:5). That is your identity.

Conclusion

Indulging your passions will lead only to greater suffering, for you and those around you. While you are uniquely you, the passions raging within you are not unique to you. "No temptation has overtaken you that is not common to man. God is faithful, and He will not let you be tempted beyond your ability, but with the temptation He will also provide the way of escape, that you may be able to endure it" (1 Corinthians 10:13). Christ's Passion is the death of your own passions. The disciplines He counsels us to take up—fasting, prayer, and works of mercy—subjugate the body, orienting us away from our own desires toward God and our neighbor. Jesus Christ is Lord and conqueror of the demons, and He will help you also battle the demons.

REFLECTION QUESTIONS

1. What are the different ways the term *passion* is used?

2. Should we strive to be *passionate*?

3. How does one passion connect to others?

4. What spiritual disciplines does Jesus give us in the Sermon on the Mount?

5. Where does the devil attack us?

6. How does a Christian find his identity?

CHAPTER 11

BATTLING YOUR DEMONS

Introduction

This chapter addresses the lifelong battle against the devil, the world, and our sinful flesh. Jesus told how an exorcised man whose house is not furnished (Luke 11:24–26) can show us the danger of underestimating the power of the devil and our own spiritual lethargy. The new life of the disciple of Jesus is built up by establishing new habits that keep furnishing and renovating the house built on the Word of God.

Demons Lie

Dark, diabolical, demonic forces are at work in the world. If you have eyes to see, the devil is the ghostwriter of congressional bills and the opinion pages of major newspapers. He tweets constantly, and his TikToks instantly go viral. What could be more opposed to the Creator than the attempt to overthrow His created order by destroying marriage, family, and the love of all human life?

The plot to destroy the Creator's intent is going on at a cosmic level, but it also is happening within you. Your heart is a throne. Who reigns there? God made us to receive life from Him. In His dominion over us, He would give us the gladness and freedom we were meant to enjoy.

The devil, on the other hand, is a liar. He tells us that God's good, creative purpose is in fact evil. "You will be like God." The devil tells us that we can only be happy by liberating ourselves from God and creation. Presenting it as enlightened science, the devil points to the deep order and design in the universe and declares, "It's all a random accident. The world is without meaning, and you are without purpose." He says, "Your body is a prison. Mutilate it, create for yourself a new identity." But of course, there is no creation there, only destruction. That is how you can identify the works of the devil: wherever there is a disruption of the created order, there you see the works of the devil.

Some things really are black and white. There is light or darkness, good or evil. Norman Nagel had it right: When it comes to life and death, right and wrong, "There is no third possibility, no middle ground, no neutral. It is unrelenting war, Satan against God, and the battleground is the human heart."[89] Satan's purpose is "to overthrow the works of God."

While the Gospels show us a suffering Jesus who submits to the cross and all the wickedness of men, another side of Jesus is also present: Jesus the warrior, the stronger man who assaults the devil's stronghold. In one parable of Jesus, the devil is likened to a warlord (a "strong man"). He says, "When a strong man, fully armed, guards his own palace, his goods are safe; but when one stronger than he attacks him and overcomes him, he takes away his armor in which he trusted and divides his spoils" (Luke 11:21–22).

The spoils of war means the plunder, the treasures that are captured and taken from the defeated enemy. The Bible presents the devil as a tyrant, a vicious totalitarian who rules the world. He holds onto the humans that God created and delights in their corruption and destruction. But Jesus is the stronger one who exorcizes the devil. Jesus goes into the devil's stronghold and takes his treasure, his spoils. What are the spoils of this war? You are. Jesus

---

89   Norman Nagel, *Selected Sermon of Norman Nagel: From Valparaiso to St. Louis* (St. Louis: Concordia Publishing House, 2004), 94.

does not come to oppress you but to liberate you, to free you for what you were meant to be.

How does the Lord Jesus accomplish this? God steps into our place as a man and accepts man's punishment. One of the great chapters of the Bible that describes this is Isaiah 53:10–12:

> Yet it was the will of the LORD to crush Him; He has put Him to grief. . . . By His knowledge shall the righteous one, My servant, make many to be accounted righteous, and He shall bear their iniquities. Therefore I will divide Him a portion with the many, and He shall divide the spoil with the strong, because He poured out His soul to death and was numbered with the transgressors; yet He bore the sin of many, and makes intercession for the transgressors.

"He shall divide the spoil"—Isaiah describes the suffering of Jesus as a victorious battle. You are the spoils of war; your new life is God's aim. So Jesus doesn't *only* want to forgive you. He wants to liberate you. In His work of driving the devil away, Jesus says, "The kingdom of God has come upon you" (Luke 11:20).

What does that mean? In his Small Catechism explanation of the Second Petition of the Lord's Prayer, Luther gives a very helpful summary of God's kingdom: "God's kingdom comes when our heavenly Father gives us His Holy Spirit, so that by His grace we believe His holy Word and lead godly lives here in time and there in eternity." Believe God's Word; lead godly lives. St. Paul's Letter to the Ephesians spells out what that means for you: Imitate God by walking in love. That means some things have to go in your life.

> But sexual immorality and all impurity or covetousness must not even be named among you, as is proper

among saints. Let there be no filthiness nor foolish talk nor crude joking, which are out of place, but instead let there be thanksgiving. For you may be sure of this, that everyone who is sexually immoral or impure, or who is covetous (that is, an idolater) has no inheritance in the kingdom of Christ and God. (Ephesians 5:3–5)

The baptized person who persists in these sins is like the man Jesus told about who is freed from the power of the devil, his house is swept and put in order, but it is never adorned and guarded with the cross. "And the last state of that person is worse than the first" (Luke 11:26).

Do not be deceived: the devil is real, demons are real, and they want to destroy your life. Their primary work is effected not through terrifying cinematic effects but by telling lies.

The Lie of Scientism

In the battle against modern philosophy, Christianity is seen as—and sometimes *is*—in a battle with the modern world itself. Modernity sees Christianity as mired in antiquated superstition. One can talk about a man "battling his demons" if he is, say, an alcoholic. People understand those demons to be metaphorical.

The modernist creed is not "I believe in God, the Father Almighty" but "I believe in science." Invocation of science ends the possibility of further discussion. But not everything called science really is. *Scientism* as a worldview is quite different from the scientific method, which proposes and tests theses to understand how the physical world operates.

The more one understands these scientific laws, the greater the difficulty in denying the orderly structure of everything from the motion of planets to the circulation of blood in the human body. Examining the human genome and observing how our human characteristics are coded suggests the existence of a coder. It appears that someone coded the first humans and we have inherited the coding. Yet much of what passes for science is not physics but metaphysics. Those who follow the philosophy of scientism, having rejected God, must supply someone else to have done the coding, including aliens.[90] The religion of scientism doesn't want you to know its secret: if there is no God, we'll have to invent one with a different name. In this religion, there is room for aliens but not for angels or demons. That is the false dogma taught in the temples of scientism.

In this faux religion, people are basically good, and there is no innate or inherent evil, much less evil spirits. The dream of twentieth-century progressive education was that we could create a utopian society if we simply educated people sufficiently. The temperance movement was going to improve society by getting rid of alcohol. The eugenics movement was going to improve society by ridding the world of bad genes. This gave rise in America to an obsession with birth control and abortion, and the self-same ideology drove the National Socialists (Nazis) to murder by the millions those of so-called inferior races.

That is evil. The Allied powers fought this evil in the Second World War. The evil was seemingly vanquished, but it lives on. Anti-Semitism is on the rise and major government leaders advocate infanticide, yet it seems like no one fights against these wrongs. That inaction is also evil.

None of this is political in the partisan sense. The task of

---

90 Some advocates of scientism, having excluded God as a possibility, posit a theory called *directed panspermia*, whereby aliens "seeded" our planet with life, which then grew and evolved. See Thomas Nagel, *Mind and Cosmos: Why the Materialist Neo-Darwinian Conception of Nature Is Almost Certainly False* (New York: Oxford University Press, 2012).

theology is not in persuading you how to vote. This principle comes first in Christian reflection on politics: "Put not your trust in princes" (Psalm 146:3). What I want you to do, dear reader, is embrace this proposition: *Evil exists.* We can't educate, medicate, or psychologize our way out of that problem.

Evil Exists

Evil exists. And there are beings that are evil. Personal beings. Some of these evil creatures we call demons. You do not need to be superstitious, or an uneducated rube, to believe that. From our first parents to Jesus Himself, we have the accounts of those who have confronted Satan.

None of this has the same sensationalism shown in movies about demonic possession. Those kinds of things can happen, but most of the devil's work is of a more ordinary sort. He is anti-human. The devil hates us and wants us to destroy one another. War and murder are great ways to do that, but so are all the other things that eventually lead to wars, such as lies, adultery, thefts, oppression, and deception. The devil does not need you to join some satanic cult if he can get you to hate the person in the next pew. Whatever will drive you away from trust in Jesus and into pride or despair, that is the demon's goal.

But "the reason the Son of God appeared was to destroy the works of the devil" (1 John 3:8). We are in the fight of our lives, not only with the devil, but also with the world and our own sinful nature. I always feel it during the penitential seasons of the Church Year. Whenever I try to return to a greater devotion to God's Word and self-discipline, evil assaults intensify. Perhaps you have experienced that too.

The earthly ministry of Jesus was a battle against the devil.

Exorcism characterized Jesus' ministry. Gospel accounts will state this in a very plainspoken way: "Now He was casting out a demon that was mute" (Luke 11:14). The devil assaults human life, often in seemingly "ordinary" ways, like damaging a person's mind or body. Sometimes the demons we hear about did wild things, like the boy who threw himself in the fire (Matthew 17:15). Others are what we would think of as merely ailments or sicknesses. Not everything is possession or habitation of a person's mind or body. But everything demonic is arrayed against God's gift of human life and His Gospel gift of the forgiveness of sins and the promise of resurrection.

When Jesus calls us to fast, pray, give alms, and meditate on the Word (Matthew 6:1–18; 7:24), He is preparing us for our own battle against the devil and our own sinful nature. The accounts in the Gospels of Jesus' victory over the devil (e.g., Matthew 4:1–11) are for our encouragement in the battle. There we learn that the demons are put to flight by the work of Jesus. For us, this means the demons are put to flight by God's Word and the Sacraments.

Only Jesus has the power to overcome the devil. Satan wants to destroy the human race. But Jesus has already won the battle in willingly dying, as both the punishment for sin and as the man who trusted God the Father to raise Him from death. Yet when Jesus teaches us about His victory over the devil, it is followed by a warning. A man freed from the devil can fall prey again. Jesus teaches,

> When the unclean spirit has gone out of a person, it passes through waterless places seeking rest, and finding none it says, "I will return to my house from which I came." And when it comes, it finds the house swept and put in order. Then it goes and brings seven other spirits more evil than itself, and they enter and dwell

> there. And the last state of that person is worse than
> the first. (Luke 11:24–26)

The liberated man's house was emptied of its demonic inhabitants but then never furnished. The doors were not locked; there was no security. So the house was broken into. Jesus says the last state of that man was even worse than before.

Can that happen to us? It certainly can. So what do we do? We go back to the work and Word of Jesus. That is where we live. Baptism drives the devil away; the name of Jesus drives the devil away; the Word of God drives the devil away.

You may have seen yard signs or window stickers for homes equipped with security services: "Protected by Acme." That is what the sign of the holy cross is for us. The Lord puts His mark on you and says, "Protected by Jesus, redeemed by His holy cross."

I once was going through a security screening with my clerical collar on. The security officer apologized to me, saying he wished he did not have to screen me. He quoted a Bible passage, "Touch not the Lord's anointed" (a paraphrase of Psalm 105:15), an Old Testament passage about not harming the king of Israel that sometimes gets applied to pastors. This kind man's conscience told him not to check me, but his job required it.

As I put my shoes back on, collected my things, and thought about how nice that man was, I got a new insight into that passage. In the New Testament, the Lord's anointing is not something special for pastors. The anointing applies to every baptized child of God. Those who are old, young, at work, homebound, in Mensa, intellectually disabled, the life of the party, socially awkward—all are special and precious to the Lord Jesus. When you were baptized, the Lord put His anointing on you. He says to the devil, "Touch not My anointed! For this person is in Christ" (a title that means "Anointed One").

When you were baptized, you were given the greatest gift. The Lord made you His temple. Your body is His temple. His temple is no place for foul speech, anger, or lies. His temple is no place for adultery or pornography. His temple is no place for pride or despair.

If you have fallen to these sins or others, do not despair. Confess your sins and run to where the Word of God is proclaimed. The message of the forgiveness of sins cleanses you, His temple, anew. Evil is driven out of the house by the Word of the Lord, by the name of Jesus, by the Lord's Supper. This work Jesus does—driving the devil away—continues wherever the Word is preached and the name of Jesus is proclaimed.

It is not superstitious to believe that evil exists, to believe that there really are demons. The world may count it weird, but that's okay. So what? But even more than that, we believe, teach, and confess that Jesus has overcome the devil. You can trust in Him. Jesus will deliver you from every evil and bring you to the resurrection of the body and the life of the world to come. Until the Last Day, keep watch so that you do not fall away. For the devil still prowls about like a roaring lion, seeking whom he may devour (1 Peter 5:8).

Keeping Watch for Sin

In the controversy between Cain and Abel over worship (Genesis 4:3–5), the Lord warns Cain that he has an enemy: "If you do not do well, sin is crouching at the door. Its desire is contrary to you, but you must rule over it" (v. 7). Sin is likened to an animal lying at the door. This animal is deceptive in that while the person is committing the sin, the animal seems friendly, tame, and docile.

There is no danger. Only after the sin is indulged does the beast reveal its true nature. He was not asleep at all but was lying in wait to devour the man. Luther compares this to a greedy man who sees the opportunity for treasure, or an adulterer who has an opportunity to be with another man's wife. At the moment of grasping the object of desire, he does so "with the idea that there can be no limit or end to the pleasure."[91] Only afterward is there a realization of the damage done. Is that realization repentance—or merely lust temporarily satiated?

This passage is given to us not simply to record God's conversation with Cain but also for our instruction, that we might know the deceptive power over sin. In the military, snipers are trained how to make ghillie suits from the target environment, to blend in with the grasses, bushes, or whatever the landscape. They must spend hours moving at a snail's pace, attempting to avoid detection from other trained snipers searching for them with binoculars. Sin is like this. It creeps into our environment and sneaks up on us who are unsuspecting. Christian poets long have warned us about this:

Rise, my soul, to watch and pray;
From your sleep awaken!
Be not by the evil day
Unawares o'ertaken;
For the foe,
Well we know,
Is a harvest reaping
While the saints are sleeping.[92]

I walk in danger all the way.
The thought shall never leave me

---

91 Martin Luther, *Luther's Works*, American Edition, vol. 1: *Lectures on Genesis: Chapters 1–5*, ed. Jaroslav Jan Pelikan, trans. George V. Schick (St. Louis: Concordia Publishing House, 1958), 267.

92 Johann Burkhard Freystein, "Rise, My Soul, to Watch and Pray" (*LSB* 663:1).

That Satan, who has marked his prey,
Is plotting to deceive me.
This foe with hidden snares
May seize me unawares
If I should fail to watch and pray.
I walk in danger all the way.[93]

Satan marking his prey is precisely the image given to Cain, and us, in Genesis 4. Like that sniper or an assassin, sin comes upon us. It offers pleasure but gives us poison. "What happened to Cain happens to everybody."[94] Hiding at the door, sin is positioned to assault us in a place where we must go. Some have made the mistake of thinking that they can escape sin by retreating from the world (e.g., to a monastery), but sin finds us wherever. Whatever our doorway is, there sin will be, preparing to strike.

This does not mean we should put ourselves in a position to sin. A pastor once presented this case to a group of pastors for consultation: a man who needed a job had found employment at a nightclub that had nude dancers. Should he keep the job? My answer was a resounding "No!" We don't put ourselves in a position to sin. The pastor who confirmed me said words I will never forget: "If you don't want to fall into the well, don't go near the edge." Later when I went off to college, he wrote me a letter (he was a good pastor) encouraging me to choose my new friends carefully. He cited the passage, "Do not be deceived: 'Bad company ruins good morals'" (1 Corinthians 15:33). I can imagine some calling this moralistic, but it is in the Bible.

We certainly should put ourselves in situations and be with people that will not tempt us to sin. Nevertheless, sin will find us

---

93   Hans Adolf Brorson, "I Walk in Danger All the Way" (*LSB* 716:1).
94   Martin Luther, *Luther's Works,* vol. 1, 267.

wherever we are. We must keep watch for it. "Wake up from your drunken stupor, as is right, and do not go on sinning" (1 Corinthians 15:34). Thus did the Lord speak to Cain, and to us, with the warning about sin crouching at the door.

Keep watch, for sin means to engage in a spiritual battle. "For if you live according to the flesh you will die, but if by the Spirit you put to death the deeds of the body, you will live" (Romans 8:13). The life of the Christian is a never-ending conflict between the new man and the old, sinful nature. To each temptation, the disciple of Jesus says to his flesh, "I refuse to obey." This is what it is to "rule over" the sin. Luther's beautiful lecture on this passage reminds us of the context, namely, the promise of the Messiah (the "Seed" of Genesis 3:15), who will crush the head of the serpent. In this way, the exhortation to battle sin has both fear and trust, Law and Gospel. To this Luther wrote, "Thus the exhortation is very rich in comfort; for on account of the blessed Seed we are no longer under the domination of sin. Therefore we should rule over sin. At all events, the exhortation gives expression to two doctrines, one dealing with fear and the other with faith. We should fear God because sin lies at the door; and we should trust God because He is merciful."[95]

Keeping Watch over Your Eyes

The battle against sin means not only to watch with our eyes but also to watch over our eyes. Watching your eyes means keeping a constant guard against what you allow into your mind through visual stimuli. Once the corrupting influences have been seen, they are not easy to remove. The holy prophet Job says, "I have made a covenant with my eyes; how then could I gaze at a virgin?" (Job

---

95   Martin Luther, *Luther's Works*, vol. 1, 270.

31:1). He has decided beforehand what he will do when confronted with an alluring image: not *gaze*, that is, continue to look with lust. You cannot always help what you see, but once you see it, you have a choice: renounce the thoughts it suggests or continue to meditate on the image. This is true whether it is something you see in person, on television, or on a website.

This is true not only of sexually suggestive images but also of anything that can provoke sin. Social media particularly presents an unreal life that creates dissatisfaction with our own. Few people post images of themselves at their worse: disheveled, unwashed, in an unkempt house. Everything is carefully curated to present the ideal image. Those images suggest that everyone is having more fun than you, is experiencing greater success than you, and is healthier, wealthier, and happier than you. It's a lie. Coveting with your eyes your neighbor's vacation, meal, or family is only making you miserable—and discontent with what God has given you. Remove it from your life. Say, "I will not set before my eyes anything that is worthless" (Psalm 101:3). This is difficult to do! It requires more than self-control; it requires prayer, as we ask for the things God has commanded: "Turn my eyes from looking at worthless things; and give me life in Your ways" (Psalm 119:37).

Aesthetic pleasure was part of the first temptation. Eve saw that the forbidden tree "was a delight to the eyes" (Genesis 3:6). She believed the devil's twisted offer that eating it would open her own eyes (v. 5). Gazing on the object of desire, her eyes were opened, to be sure—opened to the horror of death and corruption.

The Lord's antidote to this was not to look at nothing but to look upon that which brings His deliverance to remembrance. His Passover "shall be as a mark on your hand or frontlets between your eyes" (Exodus 13:16). In the puritanical-influenced American religious environment, things like crucifixes and sacred art are often discouraged in churches and homes.

I believe, however, we need to set these things before our eyes to keep us from being distracted and also to remind us of our confession of faith. When I travel, I carry in my suitcase a little picture of Jesus; He has a cross behind Him and a sheep on His shoulders, evoking the lost sheep of Luke 15:3–7. It says in Greek, "The Shepherd, the Noble One" (i.e., the Good Shepherd). I find that temptations abound when traveling, even if it's just the self-destructive temptation to stay up late. The little picture that I put out reminds me that the hotel room filled with saccharine images and the meaninglessness of contemporary existence is redeemed by Christ. He sanctifies this place and everywhere else I must go. But I dare not go without Him. Of course, the picture is not Jesus, nor is it a magic totem to ward off evil, but the image preaches to me my need for Him—and His desire to help. It invites me to pray.

Similarly, the sacrifices in the Hebrew tabernacle, and the symbols and paraments in our churches, point us to the reality that triumphs over the filtered pixelated images that offer us temporary pleasure but leave us with only regret. The psalmist saw how well the evildoers prospered, and it led him to grief: "But as for me, my feet had almost stumbled, my steps had nearly slipped. For I was envious of the arrogant when I saw the prosperity of the wicked" (Psalm 73:2–3). Seeing—literally seeing—the Lord's work in His house gave the psalmist the vision of reality that scatters the temporal image of the wicked prospering: "But when I thought how to understand this, it seemed to me a wearisome task, until I went into the sanctuary of God; then I discerned their end" (vv. 16–17).

When evil things, or bitter things masquerading as sweet, cloud our eyes, there is one thing to do: look at what is good, true, and beautiful in the cross and resurrection of Jesus, and all the things in the history of the church's art that proclaim Him to us.

Keeping Watch over Your Mouth

An order of evening prayer we often use at my church contains this prayer drawn from Psalms: "Set a watch before my mouth, O Lord, and guard the door of my lips. Let not my heart incline to any evil thing; let me not be occupied in wickedness with evildoers."[96] This prayer recognizes that, as with the eyes, self-control by itself is not enough. The Lord's help is needed, and while the mouth is the door, the heart is the home. The heart is the source of the problem.

In a controversy over food and fasting, Jesus said that what comes out of the mouth is more reflective of pollution than what goes in. "Do you not see that whatever goes into the mouth passes into the stomach and is expelled? But what comes out of the mouth proceeds from the heart, and this defiles a person. For out of the heart come evil thoughts, murder, adultery, sexual immorality, theft, false witness, slander. These are what defile a person. But to eat with unwashed hands does not defile anyone" (Matthew 15:17–20). The heart is by nature defiled and filled with evil. We are born this way (Psalm 51:5). Only the rebirth from above can change us (John 3:5). Yet our heart still has these impulses, tendencies, and passions (Romans 7:18–19). Like a raging monster eager to be let out of its cage, the heart wants to control the mouth and speak words of poison, Wormtongue filling our interlocutors' ears with lies, gossip, slander, and the like.

It seems best, then, to be slow to speak and quick to listen (see James 1:19), for opening the mouth brings destruction. "Whoever guards his mouth preserves his life; he who opens wide his

---

96   *LSB*, p. 246; cf. Psalm 141:3–4.

lips comes to ruin" (Proverbs 13:3). Yet there does come a time to speak, and for this, we pray that God does the speaking through us. After David's great sin with Bathsheba—in which David committed adultery with her, attempted to cover it up, and finally murdered her husband, Uriah—the prophet Nathan confronted him (2 Samuel 11–12). David's prayer of confession has him pleading for forgiveness. He is, as it were, reduced to silence from his own boasting and his own exercising of the kingship. The only thing he can mouth is contrition and repentance. The absolution alone will open his mouth and teach him to speak aright. "Deliver me from bloodguiltiness, O God, O God of my salvation, and my tongue will sing aloud of Your righteousness. O Lord, open my lips, and my mouth will declare Your praise" (Psalm 51:14–15). In the Western tradition, that last sentence has been the opening for numerous offices of daily prayer.[97] Anytime you are preparing to speak publicly, or anticipating a difficult conversation, saying, "O Lord, open my lips, and my mouth will declare Your praise" is a great way to pray, as is this verse, "Let the words of my mouth and the meditation of my heart be acceptable in Your sight, O Lᴏʀᴅ, my rock and my redeemer" (Psalm 19:14).

Keeping Watch over Your Time

As we'll discuss further in the final chapter, Scripture warns us that "it is the last hour" (1 John 2:18). While the ancients lived for many centuries, the increasing corruption of the world began to diminish man's lifespan. In the only psalm attributed to Moses (who himself lived to 120 years), the typical lifespan is described as seventy or eighty years:

---

97   The offices are orders of prayer for specific times of day, consisting of Psalms, Scripture readings, prayers for the time of day and year, along with other devotional material. Examples include Matins for morning prayer, Vespers for afternoon or evening prayer, and Compline for before bedtime.

All our days pass away under Your wrath;
    we bring our years to an end like a sigh.
The years of our life are seventy,
    or even by reason of strength eighty;
yet their span is but toil and trouble;
    they are soon gone, and we fly away.
Who considers the power of Your anger,
    and Your wrath according to the fear of You?
So teach us to number our days
    that we may get a heart of wisdom. (Psalm 90:9–12)

The old Latin expression *Tempus fugit,* "time flies," captures this psalm perfectly. Seventy or eighty years seems like a very long time when one is young, but as the years mount into decades, as friends die and our own endurance diminishes, we become aware that our time is short.

There is a modern attempt to domesticate death; many churches, taking their cue from the mortuaries, no longer have funerals but "celebrations of life." Such events are necessarily backward-looking, with pictures and videos from when the person was younger, favorite songs, and stories of remembrance. An anemic notion of passing on to a "better place" is referenced, and any possibility of judgment is denied. It is not wrong, of course, to remember the person, to give thanks for the good things we received from him or her. The danger is in pretending that death is a light thing and denying what God says about it.

For death itself is judgment. That is the hard truth with which Psalm 90 confronts us. "All our days pass away under Your wrath. . . . Who considers the power of Your anger?" The time we live in now is under the all-seeing eye of the Judge, and the time is short. Well-meaning "celebrations of life" are not teaching what

Moses prays for: "Teach us to number our days." We are not to think of the seventy or eighty years as a limit or a guarantee, but to recognize there is a limit. We do not know when our last hour will come, and we need to live with a view to the shortness of our time and the coming judgment. Luther wisely comments, "Grant us to know that our days are transitory and measurable."[98] The measurability of the days is mentioned not so we would attempt to divine how long our life is in this world but so we would recognize that life's end may be at any moment. We are frail. We are summoned to the old custom of *memento mori*, daily preparation for death, and so pray, "O LORD, make me know my end and what is the measure of my days; let me know how fleeting I am!" (Psalm 39:4). The great English hymnwriter Thomas Ken, in his evening hymn, taught us to cheerfully prepare for death in the confidence of Christ at the end of each day:

Teach me to live that I may dread
The grave as little as my bed.
Teach me to die that so I may
Rise glorious at the awe-full day.[99]

Knowing that our time is short, we want to spend each day faithfully laboring in our vocations, making the best use of our time. "Look carefully then how you walk, not as unwise but as wise, making the best use of the time, because the days are evil" (Ephesians 5:15–16). St. Paul uses the same phrase in Colossians 4:5: "Walk in wisdom toward outsiders, making the best use of the time." The phrase "making the best use of" is sometimes translated as "redeeming [the time]," which gets closer to the sense of the Greek term St. Paul uses (*exagorazomenoi*), which connotes going

98   *Luther's Works*, American Edition, vol. 11, *First Lectures on the Psalms 2, Psalms 76–126*, ed. Hilton C. Oswald, trans. Herbert J. A. Bouman (St. Louis: Concordia Publishing House, 1976), 205.
99   *LSB* 883:3.

to market or going out to buy. The nuance is to "buy time," not in the sense of stalling or trying to gain more time for yourself, but in getting everything you can out of the time given. This is coupled with a special word for time in Greek, *kairos* (as opposed to *chronos*, as in our words *chronological* and *synchronize*). *Kairos* is a limited period of time that is also often the opportune time, a decisive time. Think of the Latin phrase often used in motivational speeches, *carpe diem*: "Seize the day!" This is the time-management advice of St. Paul, not for the purpose of becoming more successful for yourself, but to see your time as the time God has chosen for you to act. He put you at this specific time for His purpose. It may be to change your baby's diapers, change your neighbor's tire, or change your church's theology from weak to strong in biblical doctrine. Wherever you have been placed, use the time, buy it up, and spend it on living out God's calling to you in the fullest.

It won't be easy. "For we do not wrestle against flesh and blood, but against the rulers, against the authorities, against the cosmic powers over this present darkness, against the spiritual forces of evil in the heavenly places. Therefore take up the whole armor of God, that you may be able to withstand in the evil day, and having done all, to stand firm" (Ephesians 6:12–13).

The Terrors of the Night

You will not fear the terror of the night. (Psalm 91:5)

A young man just out of college lived alone for the first time in his life. The nighttime became unbearable for him. The things he feared, manageable in the daylight, overwhelmed him in the darkness. Losing sleep made him unproductive and unstable. The words that his mother often spoke to him in his youth became his solution: "Pray the Psalms." Psalm 27 became the means by which he found sleep:

> The LORD is my light and my salvation;
>> whom shall I fear?
> The LORD is the stronghold of my life;
>> of whom shall I be afraid?
> When evildoers assail me
>> to eat up my flesh,
> my adversaries and foes,
>> it is they who stumble and fall.
> Though an army encamp against me,
>> my heart shall not fear;
> though war arise against me,
>> yet I will be confident.
> One thing have I asked of the LORD,
>> that will I seek after:
> that I may dwell in the house of the LORD
>> all the days of my life,
> to gaze upon the beauty of the LORD
>> and to inquire in His temple.
> For He will hide me in His shelter
>> in the day of trouble;
> He will conceal me under the cover of His tent;
>> He will lift me high upon a rock. (Psalm 27:1–5)

The rhetorical questions in the opening verse expect the answer "No one." The Lord is not simply "lord" in the abstract; He is *my* Lord. This is the brilliant insight of Luther's Small Catechism. With each person of the Trinity mentioned in the Apostles' Creed, Luther confesses not just the work of the Father, Son, and Holy

Spirit but also how that work is connected to the individual. Thus, in the First Article, "I believe that God has made *me* . . ." In the Second Article, "I believe that Jesus Christ . . . is *my* Lord." And in the Third Article, "I believe that . . . the Holy Spirit has called *me* by the Gospel." Thus, in the dark hours of the night, the disciple of Jesus can confess, "This Jesus is *my* Lord. He is my stronghold against everything I fear. Even evildoers and armies have no power against me. He will hide me, He will conceal me, He will lift me up above my enemies. Therefore, 'In peace I will both lie down and sleep; for You alone, O LORD, make me dwell in safety' (Psalm 4:8)."

This way of praying the Psalms is not a matter of saying the right words once. It is no mere psychological technique to find comfort. Saying back to God the words He has given us has the deeper result of inwardly digesting those words such that they become part of our soul. God's Word shapes what we think, becoming our way of approaching every situation in life. Thus, we even have images in the Scripture of "eating" the Word (Ezekiel 3:1–3; Revelation 10:9–10).

At my family's bedtime prayers, we customarily sing the ancient hymn "Before the Ending of the Day" (*LSB* 889). With only four musical notes, it is very easy to sing, and it powerfully prays for God's protection against night's terrors:

Before the ending of the day,
Creator of the world, we pray!
Thy grace and peace to us allow
And be our guard and keeper now.

From all the terrors of the night,
From evil dreams defend our sight;
Drive far away our wicked foe
That stain of sin we may not know.

O Father, this we ask be done
Through Jesus Christ, Thine only Son,
Who with the Holy Ghost and Thee
Both lives and reigns eternally. Amen.

Interestingly, the "evil dreams" of stanza 2 are not just nightmares. The original Latin has *noctium phantasmata*, "nocturnal phantasms." A phantasm can be a ghostly apparition, a mental image, or a fantasy. When this is combined with the last line in that stanza regarding "that stain of sin," the meaning starts to become clearer. The original of that last line has *polluantur corpora*, "bodily pollution." My suspicion is that the monks who originally sang this song at bedtime recognized night's great challenge: try as one may to lead a righteous, celibate life during the daytime, during the night the base desires overwhelmed mind and body with dreams of illicit sexual encounters. The resultant stain was no metaphor.

This raises the question "Can a dream be a sin?" The temptation is to answer no. After all, how can I be held responsible for what happened while I was sleeping? Yet the doctrine of original sin reveals to us the ugly truth: there is more happening with me than my waking rational mind. Those desires of the subconscious mind, corrupted as they are by concupiscence, indicate the deep disorder in my soul. Thus, the church's songs teach us to pray for protection for when our guard is down through sleep, not only from external foes who may strike but also from the internal foe that is our sinful nature. The same songs also teach us that when we do sin, while sleeping or awake, we can ask Jesus to forgive us, and He will.

In Pursuit of Virtue

In speaking of the sinful nature, one can get the impression that the entire Christian life simply consists of restraint and forgiveness of sins. While it is true that our Lord Jesus Christ willed our entire life to be one of repentance,[100] we are exhorted everywhere to pursue a holy life. Luther himself was cautious to speak about virtue, as the specific use of the term in his time could, he believed, hinder genuine good works.[101] Yet the Ten Commandments do teach us to positively pursue a faith active in love toward God and our neighbor.

A positive treatment of virtues, or good works, can provide a program for reorienting the inborn (and learned) impulses to evil toward the new life of the baptized through meditation on God's Torah. For "blessed is the man . . . [whose] delight is in the law of the LORD, and [who] on His law . . . meditates day and night" (Psalm 1:1–2).

For example, the person who is filled with anger toward his neighbor can meditate on the Fifth Commandment, "You shall not murder," and consider Luther's explanation in his Small Catechism: "We should fear and love God so that we do not hurt or harm our neighbor in his body, but help and support him in every physical need." As he considers these words, the person begins with faith that in Christ, his own sins against the commandment are absolved; then he strives to live out that absolution toward the neighbor who has offended him. Instead of calling for what he

100 Martin Luther, "Ninety-Five Theses," *Luther's Works,* American Edition, vol. 31, *Career of the Reformer 1,* trans. and ed. Harold J. Grimm, ed. Helmut T. Lehmann (Philadelphia: Fortress Press, 1957), 25.
101 Gifford A. Grobien, *Christian Character Formation: Lutheran Studies of the Law, Anthropology, Worship, and Virtue,* Oxford Studies in Theological Ethics (Oxford University Press, 2019), 185–92.

perceives as justice—the punishment of the one who angers him—
he calls for mercy and strives to implement that mercy in his own
life, helping and supporting the offending neighbor in his bodily
needs.

For the man whose lust is at war within him, he can likewise
meditate on the Sixth Commandment, "You shall not commit
adultery." The virtue of chastity is in remaining faithful to his wife
and orienting his sexual love toward her and her alone, while recognizing that her body is not simply an object for the satiation of
his lust but a temple of the Holy Spirit to be revered. So he re-
cites (out loud, if possible, but if not, in his mind) over and over a
meditation based on Luther's Small Catechism explanation of the
commandment: "We should fear and love God so that we lead a
sexually pure and decent life in what we say and do, and husband
and wife love and honor each other." The man does this until his
mind can distinguish between momentary lust and vocation. As
his mind urges him to desecrate his eyes, soul, and body by making
another woman the object of his desire, the meditation guides him
instead to focus on his wife, whom he is to love and honor. This is
more than self-control. It is more than abstaining from viewing
pornography or refraining from having an affair. It is also more
than allowing marriage to merely be the licit outlet of his burning
lust (though St. Paul does advise this as a beginning—but not an
ending—point in 1 Corinthians 7:9). The focus has shifted from
sex to love and honor. This involves conversation, compassion,
consideration, commiseration, gratitude, praise, and companionship.

Not only the Ten Commandments but also other passages of
God's Word can be used this way in the resistance of vice and the
cultivation of virtue. We see Jesus in the temptation narratives us-

ing God's Word to drive away the devil (see Matthew 4:1–11). A man who finds himself fixated on another man's wife, for example, can take up the first part of the Tenth Commandment, "You shall not covet your neighbor's wife," and repeat it to himself when the thought enters his mind. Repeating the passage can then become a prayer: "Dear Father, send down Your Holy Spirit upon me, that I may learn not to covet my neighbor's wife but rejoice in what You have given me." Or one can use a Bible narrative to shape the prayer: "Lord Jesus Christ, Son of God, have mercy on me. You did not succumb to temptation but drove away the devil. Drive the demons far from me and give me eyes to see that not even all the kingdoms of the world are worth one moment of idolatry. I thank you for the wife you have given me. Make me truly grateful for her, and strengthen me with love to be her protector, provider, helper, and friend."

Similar prayers oriented toward marriage can be said by those who are single but desire a godly wife or husband. Petitions for patience are appropriate, but bold prayers stating your desires are also fitting (always being mindful that our prayers are governed by the will of God and that our current trials are used by God for our training and discipline). "You do not have, because you do not ask" (James 4:2). The Psalms are full of prayers for every situation; I also find hymnbooks and prayerbooks filled with profound prayers to be very helpful. The Psalms teach us the language of prayer and give words to our incoherent feelings, pointing us in the direction of God. But in specific situations, I believe we must be bold and direct, asking for specific things. For example, if you are a single woman and desire to be married, then you may pray something like this: "Dear Father, send me a husband. I desire to live according to Your commandments. I want to be a godly wife and mother.

Like a forsaken desert, I see no Christian men who want me for a wife. Send me one. I am Your maidservant; I wait upon You." Then keep saying it. Will He answer? Yes. Will it be as you desire, in the timing you wish? No one but God knows. But He has promised to do for you better things than you can expect or desire. So wait upon Him, while not being anxious about anything, letting your requests be made known to Him (Philippians 4:6).

Conclusion

The devil is real. Demons are real. They rarely come with cinematic special effects. They work with words. They tell you lies. The disciple of Jesus is called to keep vigil against their assaults. What flashes before your eyes and whispers into your ears has the power to seduce you toward your own demise. Resist. You have great power to decide what you will see and what you will hear. Call upon your Jesus in the hour of trouble. He will answer and come to your help (see Psalm 50:15). He will help you subdue your passions, and He will fight the demons for you. For you fights the valiant One. "He's by our side upon the plain With His good gifts and Spirit."[102] Take heart! He is coming to re-Genesis the world.

---

102 Martin Luther, "A Mighty Fortress Is Our God" (*LSB* 656:4).

REFLECTION QUESTIONS

1. What is Satan's purpose?

2. How can the work of Jesus be called a liberation?

3. What is the difference between science and scientism?

4. What warning does Jesus give to those freed from the devil's bondage?

5. How can we rule over sin?

6. How does social media produce discontent?

7. How are the heart and mouth related?

8. How does the Bible teach us to think about time?

9. How can we use the Ten Commandments to cultivate good works in our life?

CHAPTER 12

GENESIS ALL OVER AGAIN

Introduction

God took on a body—a human body—and brought it to perfection. This Jesus, our Lord and our God, is applying to us the conversion therapy we need for our healing. He helps His disciples subdue their sinful passions and battle the demons. And in the end, He will rescue our bodies from every corruption. This great hope is the topic of our final chapter. Your destiny is not to become an angel or disembodied spirit. Christ will quite literally raise your body, and you will glorify the Father and the Lamb and enjoy the new creation freed from sinful passions. Until then, we must be ever mindful that we are living in the last hour.

It Is the Last Hour

St. John tells us, "Children, it is the last hour" (1 John 2:18). On us "the end of the ages has come" (1 Corinthians 10:11). This is the constant message to us in the New Testament. It is not meant to pinpoint the precise moment of the end of the world. It is a call for us to live our lives in the light of eternity. It is a warning to us that the day of judgment is coming.

Have you ever noticed how efficient you can be when a deadline is approaching? If I am going away on vacation, or I have to travel for work, I suddenly start reprioritizing: some things can wait but other things must get done now.

That is when I realize I should have had different priorities all along.

Why do we get a surge of dopamine when we are rewarded on social media, but turn dull and lethargic at the thought of reading God's Word? Why do we know more about the lives of actors and politicians than we know about the lives of the saints? I think we all know that when our last hour comes, we will wish we spent more time praying and less time on foolish pursuits. So why don't we act upon it now? Are we walking unawares toward disaster? "Children, it is the last hour."

In St. Paul's First Letter to the Corinthians, he tells us one of the purposes of Scripture: the narratives are a warning to us. "These things took place as examples for us, that we might not desire evil as they did" (1 Corinthians 10:6).

The continued breakdown of Western civilization reminds us that it is indeed the "last hour." The Corinthian Church needed to be wakened from their security. They lived as though there was no impending judgment. They argued. They divided into factions. They abused alcohol. They indulged their flesh. They dishonored marriage. They did not believe God could become angry with them.

As we conclude this book, now is a fitting time for self-examination. Is there reason for God to judge you? Do you live as though the last hour is far away? Do you and your church live as people who believe "the end of the ages has come" (1 Corinthians 10:11)?

The Scriptures are no mere history. They apply to us. They are "examples for us, that *we* might not desire evil" (1 Corinthians 10:6, emphasis added).

What is *evil*? Each of us has a conception of evil. But we have to step outside our own ideas and ask what is evil in God's eyes. God establishes what is good and what is evil, not the culture. God's Law shows us the eternal good in self-giving love. So the Ten Commandments are more than a list of prohibitions and requirements. They identify the eternal good: God, His name, His Word, and the way He established human life, marriage, family, our stewardship of created things, and our speech. God made us embodied creatures. "You shall not murder" reveals what is good—human life—and what is evil—death. God made us social creatures. "Honor your father and your mother" shows what is good, while "You shall not commit adultery" shows us that the foundation of the family—the permanent and selfless commitment of one man and one woman in holy marriage—is good.

Society's core problem is not immigration or the minimum wage or health care. Coming up with just the right political compromise will not bring real peace. The core problem with the world is the problem in each human heart: the desire for evil and the rejection of God's eternal good. Idolatry, fornication (in Greek, *porneia*), and grumbling all reveal that we are not living as those expecting the return of Christ.

The parable of the dishonest manager (Luke 16:1–13) shows us another form of evil—squandering the Master's goods. The Lord has appointed us to be His stewards. What has God given you that you have wasted? Have you squandered your talent or your intellect? Have you misused your time or your money? In that parable, the danger of the judgment caused a sudden change of behavior. Quickly, the steward begins to act in light of the judgment. God's Word calls us to repent quickly and live in the light of eternity. It is the last hour. On us, the end of the ages has come.

To live in the light of eternity means to reject the false views of history the world peddles. One false view of history is that time is a wheel. It teaches that all of this has happened before; all of this will happen again. We cycle through time; we get reincarnated and try again. Another false view of history is that we make progress—or evolve—toward perfection. The philosopher Hegel taught that history moves from thesis to antithesis, the struggle between the two resolving in a synthesis, which becomes the new thesis. This is popularly reflected in talk about being on the "right side of history." The Martin Luther King Jr. memorial in the District of Columbia is close to my home. It is an inspiring memorial that every American should visit. But one popular saying etched there in stone, unfortunately, reflects this Hegelian view of the world: "The arc of the moral universe is long, but it bends toward justice." The saying has its roots in the nineteenth century, adapted from Theodore Parker, a Unitarian minister, abolitionist, and Transcendentalist. While agreeing with the causes of abolition and civil rights, we cannot adopt the idea of progressive utopianism that everything in the world continues moving toward the good. Knowing that sin and death corrupt everything, we cannot place our hope in the goodness of people. It is why Christians cannot place their trust in the idea that the world can be saved through better education or social action, improved government, or fighting one more war to supposedly end all wars. We might do good—or harm—with our actions, but as Christians, we know that history has a different story and a different Savior.

In St. Paul's words that on us "the end of the ages has come" (1 Corinthians 10:11), the Holy Spirit is telling us that world history centers on Jesus Christ, on His cross and resurrection. The writer to the Hebrews tells us, "But as it is, He [Christ] has appeared once for all at the end of the ages to put away sin by the sacrifice of Himself" (9:26). In the death of Jesus, the moral arc of the universe came shooting like lightning into the Savior. In that one great cosmic event, the last age of man was ushered in. We are not building a great society; we are not building a legacy for ourselves; we are not moving history toward a perfect future. "Children, it is the last hour" (1 John 2:18), and it is given to us to repent and see in Jesus the end of the age of man. "It is finished" (John 19:30) in Jesus the perfect man.

Repent, and do not desire evil. Take heed, you who think you stand, lest you fall. Temptation has extraordinary power. You cannot stand on your own power. But as St. Paul also says in his letter to the Corinthians, "I would remind you, brothers, of the gospel I preached to you, which you received, in which you stand, and by which you are being saved, if you hold fast to the word I preached to you" (1 Corinthians 15:1–2). The Gospel—the proclamation of forgiveness and life in Jesus—is what you stand upon. So as the fire of history and the end of the world rains down upon us, as infants are torn limb from limb, as the world teeters on the brink of failure, as your body declines, and as fear sets in on every side, be not anxious! The Lord Jesus says, "Peace I leave with you; My peace I give to you. Not as the world gives do I give to you. Let not your hearts be troubled, neither let them be afraid" (John 14:27). "I have said these things to you, that in Me you may have peace. In the world you will have tribulation. But take heart; I have overcome the world" (John 16:33).

"Be watchful, stand firm in the faith, act like men, be strong. Let all that you do be done in love" (1 Corinthians 16:13–14). God will give you the power to resist your desires. "The end of all things is at hand; therefore be self-controlled and sober-minded for the sake of your prayers" (1 Peter 4:7). For what should you pray? The

Psalms give you prayers for the end of the day, the end of your life, and the end of the world: "O God, save me by Your name" (Psalm 54:1). Jesus is the incarnation, the enfleshment of God's name. The name *Jesus* means "YHWH saves" (or "YHWH is salvation"). Jesus is the answer to the prayer "O God, save me by Your name." Jesus' death is your death. Jesus' resurrection is your life.

"Children, it is the last hour" (1 John 2:18). On us "the end of the ages has come" (1 Corinthians 10:11). And that is good news! For Jesus is the resurrection and the life. He will make all things new.

The Hope of Resurrection

Much of contemporary Christianity is hamstrung with a truncated eschatology. Some people believe that after humans die, their disembodied spirit floats off to heaven, or a "better place," and that is that. A disembodied spirit is not what God made us to be. Neither do people become, as is also often supposed, angels. This false belief perhaps comes from overlooking the word *like* in these words of Jesus about marriage in the kingdom of God: "For in the resurrection they neither marry nor are given in marriage, but are *like* angels in heaven" (Matthew 22:30, emphasis added). Human beings do not become angels. Angels were created in part to be ministering spirits for humans (Hebrews 1:14). In the eschaton, Christians will judge angels (1 Corinthians 6:3).

So what is God preparing for us? Our destiny is not to be free of our body but to be clothed with a renewed, glorified body. The early Christian creeds confess this: "I believe in . . . the resurrection of the body, and the life everlasting" (Apostles' Creed); "I look for the resurrection of the dead and the life of the world to come" (Nicene Creed). One of the most ancient of the Hebrew Scriptures,

Job, teaches the resurrection of the flesh: "For I know that my Redeemer lives, and at the last He will stand upon the earth. And after my skin has been thus destroyed, yet in my flesh I shall see God, whom I shall see for myself, and my eyes shall behold, and not another" (Job 19:25–27). Job acknowledges that death will destroy his skin, yet still, he will, in his flesh, see God, in his own body with his own eyeballs. This is a tangible confession about not merely a continued existence after death but also a bodily resurrection.

Toward the conclusion of the great psalm about the crucifixion of Jesus is the joyous exultation of bodies raised from death, doing bodily things like eating and worshiping (literally, bowing down in the ancient worship posture of prostration): "All the prosperous of the earth eat and worship; before Him shall bow all who go down to the dust, even the one who could not keep himself alive" (Psalm 22:29). It is worth belaboring this point because some critical scholars allege that the Old Testament does not teach a resurrection of the body, that the resurrection is a later New Testament development. A sincere reading of the Hebrew Scriptures demonstrates otherwise.

One more example will suffice here. In Ezekiel 37, the Spirit gives the prophet comfort of future restoration for Israel in the famous "Valley of the Dry Bones" vision. Opponents of the Bible's teaching on resurrection will explain this passage away by saying it speaks merely as a metaphor for a future restoration of Israel's kingdom. There is partial truth to this, for the vision of the army that grows sinews and flesh on the reassembled skeletons is for a hopeful purpose, as the prophecy is for those who say, "Our bones are dried up, and our hope is lost; we are indeed cut off" (Ezekiel 37:11). Yet the promise is deeper than a future return to glory of Israel's descendants. The promise is specifically related to bodily resurrection, as God makes clear in the next verses: "Behold, I will open your graves and raise you from your graves, O My people. And I will bring you into the land of Israel. And you shall know that I am the Lord, when I open your graves, and raise you from your graves, O My people. And I will put My Spirit within you, and you shall live, and I will place you in your own land. Then you shall know that I am the Lord; I have spoken, and I will do it, declares the Lord" (vv. 12–14).

These opened graves are no mere resuscitation of corpses so that zombies walk the earth. The body will be transformed and glorified so that we resemble the risen Christ. "Our citizenship is in heaven, and from it we await a Savior, the Lord Jesus Christ, who will transform our lowly body to be like His glorious body, by the power that enables Him even to subject all things to Himself" (Philippians 3:20–21). In the committal rite that I use, this passage is part of the blessing of the body just before it is put into the earth. We commit the body into God's hands as we return it to the earth, confident that while the soul rests with Christ in a paradisal state (see Luke 23:43), the joyous day of resurrection will be better still.

Using picture language of a beautifully created city descending to us, St. John describes the vision he sees of a new creation: "Then I saw a new heaven and a new earth, for the first heaven and the first earth had passed away, and the sea was no more. And I saw the holy city, new Jerusalem, coming down out of heaven from God, prepared as a bride adorned for her husband" (Revelation 21:1–2). In this new creation, those whose names are written in the book of life enter the holy city and have access to the tree of life. Death is forever abolished. Over them, the second death of the final judgment has no power (Revelation 20–22).

Wilhelm Löhe imagined what we will say on the day of resurrection: "I will be able to say of that resurrected body: 'My body!' It will be a transfigured body, beaming with radiant light, a heavenly body. What a worthy companion this body, ruled over by the power of the Holy Spirit, will be to the human spirit born of God. How the soul will rejoice when it receives its old body purified, refined, and transfigured, and the power of the soul streams forth into the new body so that it moves on and over the earth, wherever it wills."[103]

There is an amazing word in the Greek New Testament whose English translation doesn't communicate its glory. The word is *palingenesia,* often translated as "regeneration" or "rebirth." The first part, *palin,* means "again." If you look carefully at the second part of the word, you can see our word *genesis.* When the two are combined, they preach a beautiful little homily of hope in one Greek word: "Genesis (all over) again." It appears in that beautiful Pauline passage on the benefits of Holy Baptism: "He saved us, not because of works done by us in righteousness, but according to His own mercy, by the washing of regeneration [*palingenesias*] and renewal of the Holy Spirit, whom He poured out on us richly through Jesus Christ our Savior, so that being justified by His grace we might become heirs according to the hope of eternal life" (Titus 3:5–7). "Genesis all over again" is what begins in Holy Baptism, but it also anticipates what God will do on the great day of resurrection, when the words of Christ reach their apex: "Behold, I am making all things new" (Revelation 21:5). This powerful word is used only one other time in the New Testament, jolting us awake to the extraordinary promise the Lord is making. In that other use, Jesus comforts His disciples, who have left everything to follow Him, by preaching to them the new Genesis: "Truly, I say to you, in the

---

103 Wilhelm Löhe, *The Word Remains* (Fort Wayne, IN: Emmanuel Press, 2016), 68.

new world [*palingenesia*], when the Son of Man will sit on His glorious throne, you who have followed Me will also sit on twelve thrones, judging the twelve tribes of Israel. And everyone who has left houses or brothers or sisters or father or mother or children or lands, for My name's sake, will receive a hundredfold and will inherit eternal life" (Matthew 19:28–29). Here our English Bible gives us the rendering "new world," but no term we have can properly describe the joy this word describes. For now, we see through a glass darkly, but then we will experience it in full (see 1 Corinthians 13:12 KJV).

Freed from the passions, we will have no envy or greed. Gone will be the lust, and we will be as our first parents, naked and not ashamed (Genesis 2:25). With the tempter cast into the lake of fire, and no concupiscence to enkindle sinful desire within us, we will be completely content with the bliss of God's new creation.

Might there be work for us to do? Not work in the sense that we think of it, as drudgery and toil. Doubtless, you know people (or perhaps you have experienced this yourself) who can spend hours upon hours working in their shop crafting things from wood. And there are those who "play hard" at perfecting their golf swing, others who devour books for the enjoyment of learning, and amateur musicians who practice a piece repeatedly for the sheer joy of making music. Our first parents had "work" to do: to be fruitful and multiply and extend Eden into the wild world. What work might the Lord set us to? We cannot say dogmatically. But we know that we will be born in a new way, regenerated, "re-Genesis-ed." There will be no sexual sin, whether heterosexual, homosexual, or any other of the ever-expanding letters in LGBTQIA+. The redeemed will be freed from the lusts that vie for power over us. All believers in Christ will be freed from the sins that haunt us. God remembers them no more (Psalm 25:7; Hebrews 8:12), and neither shall we. On that day, we will rejoice and say, "This is the day that the LORD has made; let us rejoice and be glad in it" (Psalm 118:23–24). For I am reborn this new way, by this ever-new-making God. I was dead and am alive, I was lost and am found, I was a sinner and am now holy. All praise to God, and to the Lamb, forever and ever and unto the ages of ages!

REFLECTION QUESTIONS

1. What are the greatest evils of our day?

2. What does it mean to live in light of eternity?

3. What happens after death?

4. What is the Christian's joyful expectation?

CONCLUSION

"Change and decay in all around I see; O Thou who changest not, abide with me."[104] Wearied by the changes and chances of life, it is tempting to despair. But Christ Jesus came to destroy the works of the devil. Be sober, be vigilant. He is yet with His Church, and He will not see her shipwrecked. He is the authentic man, in whom we find our calling and purpose. Because of Jesus, death has no power over you. Because of Jesus, your desires are being changed from disordered to rightly ordered. He calls you away from Narcissus's pool to stand and confess your rebirth by water and the Holy Spirit. Confess in your station the goodness of holy marriage, the sanctity of the human person and the entire human race.

Through every trial and temptation, Christ is healing you and guiding you toward your *telos*. The Holy Spirit fights for you the passions within you. The demons are put to flight. This is the last hour. Genesis is coming again. The renewal of all humanity is about to begin. In Christ will you live. In Christ will you die. In Christ will you live forever.

---

104 Henry F. Lyte, "Abide with Me" (*LSB* 878:4).